Other Books by Daniel Friedmann

Inspired Studies, Book 1: The Genesis One Code

The Genesis One Code and The Broken Gift

The author's first book, *The Genesis One Code*, demonstrates an alignment between the dates of key events pertaining to the development of the universe and the appearance of life on earth as described in Chapters 1 and 2 of Genesis, with those derived from scientific theory and observation. This book, *The Broken Gift*, follows and extends the scope of *The Genesis One Code* to include the appearance and early history of humans. Although the books stand alone and can be read in any order, reading them in the order of publication provides a comprehensive narrative starting at the beginning of the universe and proceeding until only a few thousand years ago, with all elements related from both a Biblical and scientific perspective.

INSPIRED STUDIES

BOOK 2

The Broken Gift

How did we get here?

Daniel Friedmann

Inspired Books

Printed in the United States of America.

For information contact:
INSPIRED BOOKS
www.inspiredbooks.ca

Library and Archives Canada Cataloguing in Publication

Friedmann, Daniel E. (Daniel Eduardo), 1956-
The Broken Gift: How did we get here? / Daniel Friedmann.

Includes bibliographical references and index.
ISBN 978-09784572-2-8

1. Religion and science. 2. Evolution--Religious aspects.
3. Time in the Bible   I. Title.

BL263.F75 2013   231.7'652   C2013-900610-9

ISBN: 978-0978457228

10 9 8 7 6 5 4 3 2 1

DEDICATION

To Alexandra, Zach, Michael, and Jane, who ask deep questions and are not afraid to explore answers from diverse bodies of knowledge.

TABLE OF CONTENTS

ACKNOWLEDGEMENTS...vii

FOREWORD...ix

CHAPTER 1 INTRODUCTION.................................1

The Creation Evolution Controversy.................................2
The Basis of Knowledge for Science and Religion 3
Why Science and Religion Should Agree.........................8
The Scientific Timeline for Human Origins 8
The Religion View on Human Origins............................9
Time in the Bible and Science 11
Organization of this Book.......................................13

**CHAPTER 2 DIVERGENT VIEWS: THE ORIGINS
DEBATE 17**

Scientific Inquiry...17
Beginnings..17
An Old Earth..18
Evolution 18
Genetics...19
Human Evolution..20
Creationism..21
Scientific Creationism 22
Theistic Evolution 23
Intelligent Design..24
Current Situation..24

CHAPTER 3 THE SCIENCE ANSWER 29

The Fossil Record..30
What is the Fossil Record?..30
Evidence of Life Preserved in the Fossil Record...............31
Dating the Fossil Record 31
Can We Trust the Results of Radiometric Dating?............32
The Sequence of Life Revealed in the Fossil Record...........33
Information about Humans from Buried Remains 35
Genetics...36
The Genome Projects 37
Human Timeline..38

Overview *39*
Modern Behaviors *40*
Out of Africa Migration *41*
Summary of the Human Timeline *43*
Human Speech and Language *44*

CHAPTER 4 INTERPRETING SCRIPTURES **53**

Genesis as a Valuable Information Source............................54
How Is Genesis Used to Derive Human Time for Events
Measured by Scientists?..*56*
Interpretation: The Oral Tradition 57
Midrash Rabbah...*59*
Pirkê de Rabbi Eliezer *60*
Explanations - The Commentaries 62
Rashi...*62*
Ramban...*64*
Mystical Tradition *65*
Rabbi Isaac Luria *66*
Time Conversion—Mystical Works 67
Isaac ben Samuel of Acre *67*

CHAPTER 5 CONVERSION OF TIMES.................. **71**

SECTION 1 - CREATION TIME..73
Adam and Humankind 73
The Creation Timeline 74
SECTION 2 - DIVINE TIME...77
SECTION 3 - HUMAN TIME...77
The Start Time *78*
The End Time *79*
The Human Timeline...80

CHAPTER 6 ADAM... **85**

Adam in the Garden of Eden..85
The Garden of Eden *86*
Adam...*89*
The Sin 92
The Physical Impact of the Sin on Adam and Eve....................*94*
The Spiritual Impact of the Sin on Adam and Eve....................*95*

CHAPTER 7 THE NEED FOR HUMANITY **103**

Homo Sapiens 103
Adam's Direct Descendants and Their Life Spans *106*
Homo Sapiens and Apes 107
An Intermediary *107*

CHAPTER 8 THE TIMELINE FOR THE
             APPEARANCE OF HOMO SAPIENS...111

In the Image of God 111
God's Creative Process 112
God's Names *113*
The Creative Steps *113*
A Moment *115*
The Timeline for the Sin 118

CHAPTER 9 HOMO SAPIENS: THE BIBLICAL VS.
             THE SCIENTIFIC ACCOUNT **127**

CHAPTER 10 THE FLOOD **131**

The Flood - Natural or Miraculous? 132
Description of the Flood 134
The Flood - Local or Global? 139
Midrash *140*
Derivation from the Description of the Flood *143*
The Biblical Text *144*
Does Scientific Evidence Exist for the Flood? ... 147
Mechanisms to Produce the Flood Within Nature *147*
Impact of the Flood on Human History 148

CHAPTER 11 BABEL **153**

Noah's Descendants 154
Noah's Three Sons *155*
The 70 Nations *156*
The Dispersion of Babel 156
The Scientific Record on the History of
Language 159
Summary of the History of Language: Bible
and Science 161

CHAPTER 12 CONCLUSIONS - WHERE TO FROM HERE? 165

Wave-Particle Duality 166
Free Will and Divine Providence............................. 169
Adam, His Free Will, and the Mission of Homo Sapiens.. 170
Human History 171
How Many People Have Ever Lived and Will Live On Earth?.. 172

ANNEX A GENESIS...177

Genesis 1.. 177
Genesis 2.. 178
Genesis 3.. 180
Genesis 4.. 182
Genesis 5.. 183
Genesis 6.. 184
Genesis 7.. 185
Genesis 8.. 187
Genesis 9.. 189
Genesis 10.. 191
Genesis 11.. 193

ANNEX B DIVINE TIME...195

Cycles of 7 and 49.. 195
Spiritual Cycles – the Counting of the Omer............. 195
Physical Cycles – Sabbatical Cycles for the Land....... 196
Cosmic Cycles – 49,000 Years.................................. 197
The Divine Timeline 198
The "Birth" of Adam in Divine Time 202

ANNEX C FLOOD BACKGROUND 205

Natural Flood Mechanisms....................................... 205
Cultures Surviving the Flood 209

GLOSSARY 213

INDEX 227

FIGURES

Figure 3.1 Summary of Human Migrations 43

Figure 4.1 Biblical Sources... 56

Figure 5.1 Creation Time—Day 6... 76

Figure 5.2 Timelines – Day 6 81

Figure 6.1 The Position of Continents and Garden 420Ma...... 88

Figure 8.1 Timelines of the Sin... 119

Figure 10.1 Modern Cargo Ship – Similar Size to Ark............ 139

Figure 10.2 Flood of 400 Meter Depth 142

Figure 11.1 The 70 Nations... 158

Figure 12.1 Two-slit Light Wave Interference 167

Figure 12.2 Pattern from Two-slit Interference...................... 168

Figure B.1 Creation Time and Divine Time – Day 6.............. 201

TABLES

Table 2.1 Creation vs. Evolution – Beliefs in America.............. 26

Table 3.1 Timeline for Appearance of Life on Earth.................. 34

Table 3.2 Human Timeline... 43

Table 4.1 Timeline of Biblical Sources and Persons.................. 59

Table 5.1 Human Time vs. Creation Time.............................. 78

Table 8.1 Creative Process.. 115

Table 9.1 Homo Sapiens: Biblical and Scientific Views........... 128

Table 10.1 Flood Chronology 134

Table 10.2 Dimensions – Ark vs. Other Ships...................... 139

Table 10.3 Meaning of the Hebrew Word *Erets*...................... 146

Table B.1 Seven Sabbatical Cycles................................. 200

Acknowledgements

Many people were instrumental in helping me with this work. My teachers of many years, Rabbi Avraham Feigelstock and Rabbi Shmuel Yeshayahu, introduced me to key concepts and helped me locate references.

Debra Christian provided critical editorial assistance.

Wendy Keyzer, Sol Pavony, Alan Robins and Dr. David C. Bossard provided valuable editorial comments, corrections and feedback.

I would like also to express my gratitude for the help and advice given me by my wife, Marilyn, who patiently edited, critiqued, and formatted the manuscript.

Ron V. May carefully edited the manuscript and made numerous excellent suggestions toward an essential contribution to the finished work.

Foreword

Are you educated in or otherwise well aware of the sciences and thus convinced that current scientific theories and data explain our origins? At the same time, do you have a basic awareness of Judeo-Christian scripture and its seeming incompatibility with science?

Conversely, do you believe that God created human beings and that all answers pertaining to our origins are clearly provided in scripture? At the same time, do you have a basic awareness of science and its seeming incompatibility with the teachings of your religion?

In other words, are you familiar with the main principles of both religion and science yet cannot reconcile the two to explain our origins?

At the start of this journey, I, too, was unsure whether or not the answers found in science books and religious scriptures could be reconciled. Now, having explored both in some depth, I can say that such reconciliation is not out of the question. This book attempts to demonstrate the reconciliation with respect to the appearance and early history of our species. But first, let me tell you about my background and potential biases.

I began with knowledge gained from a basic religious upbringing and a high school science education. To me, both bodies of knowledge were fascinating yet appeared incompatible. As I proceeded to obtain a scientific education, I initially came to think that science books answered everything. However, by my fourth year at university, some fundamental questions concerning human origins began to reappear. Simultaneously, in science texts some answers were not complete. So, I went back to study religion, this time also exploring the mystical component of religion so as to find deeper inner meaning rather than simple interpretation. Answers to my questions began to appear.

The Genesis creation narrative, for Christians and Jews, provides the foundation for an understanding of origins. For Muslims, too, it is an important component of the same understanding. While *The Broken Gift* is based primarily on the creation narrative, in order to delve deep into the subject's mysteries I relied on Jewish sources exclusively, since Judaism has formed the background of my religious education. Of those with different religious backgrounds, or none at all, I ask that you please continue to read on. You may find that the various sources pertaining to origins have more in common than perhaps expected. Certainly, such widely divergent narratives—the divine creation of humankind in one day less than 6,000 years ago as revealed in religious texts, versus the appearance of our species 200,000 years ago as the culmination of numerous human-like species that existed over a span of millions of years as described in scientific texts—present a key challenge. They would seem incompatible, irreconcilable. I maintain they are not.

This book presents a rigorous analysis of key events and their dates related to the appearance and early history of our species as described in both Genesis and in the latest scientific publications. No attempt is made either to discredit or excuse any body of knowledge or any particular religious belief. On the contrary, the thesis of *The Broken Gift* is that both science texts and the Bible effectively describe human origins.

Nor is an attempt made to present why bodies of knowledge or beliefs are either compatible or incompatible by providing arguments that, although potentially powerful, cannot be proved conclusively. Instead, in *The Broken Gift* every attempt is made to reconcile religion-based events and their timing relating to the appearance and early history of our species with the same events as studied by scientists. When we put aside our personal beliefs and focus only on the events and their timing, we find alignment—a startling alignment. This book aims to elucidate that squaring of supposedly irreconcilable ways of knowing. My wish is that once you have glimpsed the possibilities, you then can ponder our origins with a newly reconciled set of stories—the Biblical story, which is thousands of years old, and the scientific story, which is very new. Together, they depict the revelation of human existence itself in complementary rather than contradictory terms.

Chapter 1

Introduction

Imagine there exist manuscripts, written centuries ago, that could help us decipher the Biblical book of Genesis and thereby extract the key events and timeline recounting the appearance and early history of our species, Homo sapiens, precisely as identified by the latest scientific evidence derived from the fossil record and genetic studies.

Further, suppose these manuscripts could pinpoint the difference between modern humans, other living primates, and other extinct hominid lineages, as well as tell us when humans left Africa and when language developed as determined by ongoing scientific study.

Scientific work has shown that life emerged on earth some 3.5 billion years ago and is further theorized to have developed by a process of Darwinian natural selection, eventually evolving into the numerous species populating the earth today, including primates. Currently, evidence compiled through the scientific method has shown that Homo sapiens emerged in Africa some 200,000 years ago and remained there without significant change for more than 100,000 years. However, by 60,000 years ago Homo sapiens had developed a distinct set of modern behaviors and had left Africa to eventually spread throughout the world.

Religion, which comprises beliefs concerning the cause, nature, and purpose of the universe and humankind, is based on a personal faith in supernatural causes. For many believers, God created the universe and life in six days, with the creation of humans occurring on Day 6. And these events, moreover, are believed to have been completed at a time less than 6,000 years ago.

Scientific and religious accounts and timelines in particular would indeed seem incompatible. However, could it be these two interpretations of human origins are simply using different terms to describe the same events?

What then of these hundreds-of-year-old manuscripts? They exist, and were recently translated into English. These works can help us further interpret Genesis, the cornerstone scripture of Judaism and Christianity.

Hard to believe?

The premise of *The Broken Gift* is worth repeating: the rigorous approach of science and a careful and equally rigorous analysis of Genesis produce the same events and timelines for the appearance and early history of humanity.

The Creation Evolution Controversy

Currently, the creation-evolution controversy has pitched religion against science. Did humans appear 200,000 years ago after evolving into existence over millions of years from a chimpanzee-human common ancestor? Or, was humanity divinely created less than 6,000 years ago? If the goal of this book is achieved, we will come closer to reconciling the two approaches and solve the most contentious element of the dispute—the disagreement over the origins of humankind.

The creation-evolution controversy originated in Europe and North America in the late 18th century. Discoveries in geology led to various theories of an ancient earth, and fossils revealing past extinctions prompted early ideas of evolution. Later discoveries of fossils from extinct species, which exhibit mixtures of human and other primate features, further fueled the debate.

Recently, both sides have become more polarized in their views. Many religious believers have moved toward a fundamentalist interpretation insisting on a literal six days of creation and humanity as a divine creation. Scientists, on the other hand, adhere to a strict view of evolution as a struggle for survival among randomly mutating genes eventually leading to modern humans, with no room or need for God.

Today the general public[1] remains divided by the origins debate. Surveys indicate that half believe God specially created the first humans. Most of the rest affirm that humans developed from less advanced forms of life in a divinely guided process. Only about 15% accept the God-less origins of human life.

The Basis of Knowledge for Science and Religion

Before we can establish a correspondence in the events and timeline for human origins between science and religions that are based on the six days of creation belief, we will briefly describe the basis of knowledge for each area of study. Our scope will be to explain the scientific approach as well as the Biblical account of the beginning of human existence as we know it today.

Science is the systematic process of gathering information about the universe and organizing it into theories and laws that can be tested. To be considered scientific, a body of knowledge must pass certain objective tests. The scientific method comprises a system of processes used to establish new or revised knowledge. Moreover, a scientific approach is applied to collecting factual information. To be termed scientific, a method of inquiry must be based on gathering unbiased evidence through observation, experience, and experiment.

Of course, certain principles of reasoning and logic must be followed when one tests theories and hypotheses.

Objectivity is necessary for studies of this type. After scientific observation has been conducted, the results must be organized, summarized, and applied toward the development and testing of theories. Typically, following the process of peer review, findings are shared with an audience of qualified specialists in the field of study, as well as possibly the public at large, or some portion of it. Scientists scrutinizing a test result or theory may attempt to prove or disprove the original study's findings by reproducing the observation or experimentation under identical conditions; scientists also may perform new tests.

The scientific approach works very well when applied to extant phenomena and events. But what about events that occurred 200,000 years ago?

Amazingly, scientists today can glimpse what existed throughout the development of life on earth and, in particular, the development of our species. Nonetheless, there is no recording, written or otherwise, of what actually happened when Homo sapiens appeared, and when the species developed certain traits, like language. The only existing evidence of origins is derived from fossils, artifacts and other preserved remains from our ancestors and their environment. Therefore, in the realm of scientific inquiry we are left with continued examination of what has already been unearthed, and what is still to be discovered with constantly improving scientific methods and technologies. Accordingly, scientists and researchers continue to conduct tests on multiple hypotheses based on observation and analysis of the fossil record and living species. The current scientific consensus is that humans evolved during a span of millions of years from a chimpanzee-human common ancestor. Nevertheless, knowledge still being collected regarding the appearance and nature of our species leaves unanswered questions.

To some, this scientific body of information is inadequate, incomplete, or even inaccurate. For them, God is the architect of human life as revealed through His inspired Word in the Holy Scriptures known as the Bible. For many Christian and Jewish believers, the Five Books of Moses are considered the revealed Word of God. This means that the words contained in the Five Books of Moses, along with other scriptures and the oral tradition that elaborates and explains the Five Books, were given to Moses in the exact form we have them today, as stated toward the end of Deuteronomy (the fifth book of Moses): *"And it came to pass, when Moses had made an end of writing the words of this law in a book, until they were finished."*[2] To others, this means that God spoke to men—mainly prophets—who recorded His words in the book widely known as the Bible. Scholars estimate that the Bible was written by 40 people over a span of 2,000 years. Finally, to non-believers, the Bible is a collection of ancient myths and fables. The Bible has been translated into numerous editions, with the most widely read version likely the 1611 King James Version. Newer and more recent translations are perhaps better understood by many today, owing to the use of contemporary language rather than the early modern Elizabethan dialect that seems stilted and inaccessible to 21st-century readers.

Genesis is the first book of the Bible, and first of the five books of the law (the Pentateuch) ascribed by tradition to Moses. Beginning with the creation of the universe and humankind, the narrative relates the initial disobedience of the first man and woman, and their consequent expulsion from God's garden—Eden. Genesis, which means beginnings, contains the entire creation account. Chapter 1 of Genesis contains 31 verses describing God's acts of creating the universe and the world within a six-day period. Chapter 2 of Genesis, comprising 25 verses, elaborates on God's creation of human life in a man He called Adam, and from his side, a woman who was named Eve and who became Adam's wife. From this pair of ancestors and their children, we are told, came all human life. Chapter 3 of Genesis describes the downfall of Adam and Eve as a result of their sin. Chapters 4 through 11 relate the early human history up to the emergence of modern languages post-Babel (see Annex A for the key text relating to humans in the first 11 chapters of Genesis).

The Genesis account provides a detailed chronology of the appearance of humans and their early actions:[3]

> [1.27]*So God created man in his [own] image,*[1.28] *...and God said unto them, "Be fruitful, and multiply, and replenish the earth, and subdue it:"...*
>
> [3.6]*And when the woman saw that the tree was good for food, ... she took of the fruit thereof, and did eat, and gave also unto her husband with her; and he did eat....*
>
> [3.23]*Therefore the LORD God sent him forth from the garden of Eden, to till the ground from whence he was taken...*
>
> [6.13]*And God said unto Noah, The end of all flesh is come before me ...*
>
> [11.6]*And the LORD said, Behold, the people [is] one, and they have all one language; and this they begin to do...*
>
> [11.7]*...let us go down, and there confound their language...*
>
> [11.8]*So the LORD scattered them abroad from thence upon the face of all the earth....*

Many adherents of two major world religions—Christianity and Judaism—accept the Genesis account as factual and literal. We will more closely examine the religious implications of the Genesis account in later chapters.

The relationship between the holy books of these two religions is such that both religions share the Five Books of Moses and Psalms, in addition to other texts.

The Holy Bible, the sacred writings of the Christian religion, includes the Old Testament (containing 39 books of Hebrew scripture, including the Five Books of Moses), and the New Testament, which contains the four Gospel accounts of Jesus' life and teachings, as well as letters, mainly from the Apostle Paul, which were written to encourage and inspire new church groups that sprang up in the wake of Jesus' ministry.

For Muslims, there exists the Islamic holy book the Qur'an and other revelations, which most Muslims believe were dictated by God to various Islamic prophets. These revelations include the Tawrat (given to Moses and which is close[4] to the Five Books of Moses), the Zabur (revealed to David and close to Psalms), and the Injil (teachings revealed through Jesus). The account of creation in the Qur'an is similar in some ways to the account in Genesis. However, Islamic teaching on creation differs in critical ways. In particular, although the Qur'an does declare that creation occurred in six days, days are interpreted not as literal 24-hour hour periods but as stages or other periods of time.

Genesis is the first of the five books of the law derived from God, known as the Written Law. For Jews, the Written Law is interpreted and applied with the aid of the Oral Law, which is now documented in writing and includes the Talmud and the Zohar. The Talmud (meaning instruction or learning) is a central text of mainstream Judaism in the form of rabbinic discussions pertaining to Jewish law, ethics, philosophy, customs, and history. The Zohar (meaning splendor or radiance) is the foundational work in the literature of Jewish mystical thought; it is a group of books, including commentary, addressing the mystical aspects of the Five Books of Moses as well as matters of scriptural interpretation, while also including material on the nature of God, the origin and structure of the universe, the nature of souls, and human psychology. Together, the Written Law and the Oral Law comprise the Torah.[5]

For believers, the Torah contains legal and ethical instructions. Although not primarily intended to be a science textbook, the Torah, for those who believe it, is the revealed Word of God and presents an accurate representation of our world. In fact, the Talmudic sages teach that *"God looked into the Torah and created the world."*[6] The Torah is the blueprint of the universe's and humankind's existence from a faith-based perspective, drawn from a tradition of oral and written principles. This religious system of beliefs will be examined more closely later.

Why Science and Religion Should Agree

Thus, given that the scientific method should produce accurate descriptions of the appearance of humans, and accepting that the Torah is the blueprint for humankind's existence and human souls, as elaborated in the mystical works, key facts about the appearance of humans and their early history discussed in the Torah and determined by the scientific method should be equal. Indeed, this is the very thesis developed in detail throughout this book by means of Torah and peer-reviewed scientific sources. The answers provided by science and Torah are equal when they pertain to events and a timeline for the appearance and early history of humans— albeit the scientific and Torah explanations *of how* humanity appears are different.

How can this be?

The Scientific Timeline for Human Origins

The scientific community has synthesized the observable characteristics or traits of humans and their precursors. These have included their morphology, development, biochemical or physiological properties, behavior, and products of behavior (such as cave paintings) in order to arrive at the theory of human evolution. The scientific theory encompasses the development of the genus Homo, including the emergence of Homo sapiens as a distinct species and as a unique category of hominids (a term used to refer to humans, chimpanzees, gorillas, and their relatives) and mammals. The study of human evolution utilizes many scientific disciplines. The term "human" in the context of human evolution refers to the genus Homo, and studies of human evolution usually include earlier hominins (a term used to refer to a member of the human lineage, more closely related to living people than to chimpanzees or other living primates) such as Australopithecines (a species that was bipedal and dentally similar to humans but with a brain size not much larger than that of modern apes), from which the genus Homo is thought to have diverged about 2.3 to 2.4 million years ago in Africa.[7]

The dominant view among scientists concerning the origin of anatomically modern humans, Homo sapiens, is the hypothesis known as "Out of Africa," or recent African origin hypothesis,[8] which argues that Homo sapiens arose in Africa about 200,000 years ago and had migrated out of that continent by approximately 60,000 years ago.

The Religion View on Human Origins

Although many Christians rejected the idea of slowly-evolving humans that seemed to contradict the model of creation found in Genesis, the position of the Catholic Church on the theory of evolution has gradually been refined. For about 100 years after the publication of Charles Darwin's *On the Origin of Species* in 1859, there was no authoritative pronouncement on the subject. By 1950, Pope Pius XII had acknowledged academic freedom and agreed to the study of the scientific implications of evolution, so long as Catholic dogma was not violated. Today, the Church's unofficial position is that faith and scientific findings regarding human evolution are not in conflict. However, humans are regarded as a special creation and the existence of God is required to explain the spiritual component of human origins; the Church likewise unofficially maintains all humans descend from a single origin (i.e., the Church sees the Genesis narrative as compatible with the Out of Africa theory). Moreover, the Catholic Church teaches that the process of evolution is a planned and purpose-driven natural process, actively guided by God.[9]

Despite these accommodations, the time discrepancy between the six-day creation account and the theory of human evolution remains unresolved.

In addition, the literal Genesis account of the appearance of humans does seem very different from scientific findings. God creates Adam (albeit as we shall see later, his body and soul are made differently and at different times), and from him, Eve is made. Adam and Eve then go on to reproduce, and the rest of humanity descends from them. As we shall see later, Adam was a divine being who, as a result of the sin, became diminished, physically and spiritually. As a result, humankind, his descendants, are lesser than he. According to this account, modern humans *devolved* from a much higher spiritual being rather than, as science suggests, *evolved* from a lower physical species.

Genesis sets these events on Day 6 of creation, whereas the Biblical calendar then dates subsequent events over a period of less than 6,000 years. These science- and Bible-derived timelines lead to large apparent discrepancies for the timing of events. If we are to correlate these two very different accounts, we must reconcile the time discrepancy to allow comparison of the events and thus illuminate similarities and contradictions.

Time in the Bible and Science

Scientists have established that time has a beginning, may have an end, and is different for people within different frames of reference.[10] The Big Bang theory leads to an initial singularity from which the universe and time emerged—the beginning of time. Current theories under development[11] are disputed; however, some point to scenarios under which time, and perhaps also the universe, end. Einstein's theories of special relativity and general relativity, although counter-intuitive, show that people moving with respect to each other and/or in dissimilar gravitational fields experience time differently, and neither is absolute or universally correct. These theories have been tested and proven.

Similarly, time in the Bible has a beginning and an end, and it is different for the two conscious, separate observers of which the Bible speaks: God and man. Genesis commences from a point "in the beginning" of time. The scriptures tell us, as will be elaborated on later in this book, that the world will attain a messianic age and eventually perhaps cease to have a physical manifestation. Finally, the scriptures and their mystical interpretation reveal that time is kept differently in the physical world than in the various spiritual strata, or worlds.[12] In this respect, we are told in the Psalms that one day for God is equivalent to 1,000 years as experienced by humans.[13]

In both science and the Torah there is the concept of the conscious observer—a being observing and interpreting reality. In science, theory and experiment have revealed that the observer and his or her measurements affect the end result of an experiment in the microscopic quantum world. Recently it has been shown that quantum mechanics applies at all scales,[14] although the implications of this discovery are not yet well understood. In the Torah, these ideas definitely apply[15] to our macroscopic world; the conscious observer determines as well as causes reality. People interpret the Torah and make rulings on matters according to the law. These rulings, in turn, influence human physical reality.

We now begin to see how to correlate the Biblical timeline with the scientific one. God keeps time differently than people do. There was an earlier period in which God was the conscious observer, and a later period (still ongoing) wherein man and woman are the conscious observers. For the period when God was the conscious observer, we must convert from God's time to time as measured by humans.

This is not a modern concept. Isaac ben Samuel of Acre[16] (fl. 13th–14th century), who lived in the land of Israel 800 years ago, stated that the universe is actually billions of years old at a time when the prevalent thought was that the universe was thousands of years old. Isaac ben Samuel arrived at this conclusion by distinguishing between time as experienced by humans, and time as experienced by God, herein described as Human Time and Divine Time, respectively. However, his work was only brought to light recently in English by Rabbi Aryeh Kaplan (1979).[17]

This book attempts to establish the precise time when God was the conscious observer, and then to convert the creation events of Day 6 to Human Time. This process will allow for a precise calculation in Human Time of the Biblical timeline for the appearance of Homo sapiens; the development of modern human behaviors including language; and the human exodus from Africa to *"fill the earth."*[18] We will then examine the remaining early chapters of Genesis to extract the rest of the events and timeline relating to early human history.

With this information, and using other texts to further understand how the process occurred, we will be able to compare and contrast the scientific and Biblical accounts to reveal striking similarities in events and their timing, and also to reveal some stark disagreements, specifically *on how* humans came to be.

Organization of this Book

After the present introductory chapter, *The Broken Gift* proceeds as follows:

In Chapter 2, the historical controversy between science and religion is summarized, with emphasis on the discrepancy regarding process and timing of humankind's appearance.

In Chapter 3, the fossil record, genetics, and other scientific fields of study as they pertain to human evolution are described, including exactly what they reveal and where questions remain. This information serves as reference on the current state of scientific knowledge with regard to the appearance and early history of humans, the background allowing for comparison to similar information relating to the creation narrative as described in subsequent chapters.

In Chapter 4, the key Torah sources and authors used toward developing the interpretation of Genesis are briefly outlined. This information provides background on the Biblical references used in subsequent chapters.

In Chapter 5, a conversion of timelines is provided:

The creation timeline for Day 6 is described, and the timeframe of Adam's sin is explored.

Divine Time, or time as measured by God, is plotted on a parallel timeline showing its conversion to the creation timeline.

Human Time, or time as measured by a human being, is additionally plotted in parallel, demonstrating its conversion to Divine Time.

In Chapter 6 is described how Adam was made, what he was like, and what happened to him as a result of his sin.

In Chapter 7, why humanity was required and came into being as a result of Adam's sin is described. Also, the relation between humans and other primates from a Biblical perspective is discussed.

In Chapter 8, with the aid of the time conversion developed in Chapter 5, the events described in Chapters 6 and 7 are converted to Human Time and compared to the best scientific evidence of the appearance of humankind.

In Chapter 9, the Biblical and scientific accounts of Homo sapiens are summarized and compared.

With the Biblical and scientific evidence from the appearance of Homo sapiens 200,000 years ago until 6,000 years ago thus aligned, the two major events affecting the early history of humans, the Flood and Babel, are then explored.

In Chapter 10, the Genesis Flood and its impact on the earth and humanity is examined against scientific evidence.

In Chapter 11, the Biblical description of the spread of human language (the account of Babel) is examined against the latest studies regarding development and spread of human language.

By the time we reach Chapter 12, the book's conclusion, it will be clear that the scientific account and the Biblical account of the appearance and early history of humanity can be harnessed in tandem on identical timelines. Such apprehension of the correlation between events in the past as described by scientific evidence and Biblical teachings will bring us to a new level of understanding and further questioning of our human origins.

---

[1] Edward J. Larson, *The Theory of Evolution: A History of Controversy* (U.S.A. The Teaching Company, 2002), p. 34.

[2]   Deuteronomy 31:24, The Holy Bible, King James Version. New York: Oxford Edition: 1769; King James Bible Online, 2008. www.kingjamesbibleonline.org/.

[3]   Genesis 1:1–5, The Holy Bible, King James Version. New York: Oxford Edition: 1769; King James Bible Online, 2008. www.kingjamesbibleonline.org/.

[4]   Many Muslims believe the Judeo-Christian scriptures have been corrupted and are therefore inaccurate views of the actual revelations to Moses, David, and Christ.

[5]   The Torah comprises Written Law: Five Books of Moses, Prophets, Writings (i.e., Psalms), Sanhedrin, Rabbinical Laws and Customs; and Oral Law: Talmud (Mishna, Gemarah), Explanations, Midrashim, Zohar. All Biblical quotes and commentaries (unless otherwise referenced) are from translations found in *The Stone Edition Chumash, the Torah, Haftaros, and Five Megillos, with a Commentary from Rabbinic Writings*, General Editors Rabbi Nosson Scherman and Rabbi Meir Zlotowitz (New York: Mesorah Publications Ltd., 2009). All Talmud quotes are from the English translations found in *Soncino Babylonian Talmud*, Ed. Rabbi Dr. I. Epstein (London: The Soncino Press, 1935–1948).

[6]   Midrash Rabbah on Genesis 1:2; Zohar I:134a, Vol. II, 161b.

[7]   John Hawks, *The Rise Of Humans: Great Scientific Debates"* (U.S.A. The Teaching Company, 2011), p. 3.

[8]   Paul Mellars, "Why Did Modern Human Populations Disperse from Africa ca. 60,000 Years Ago?" *Proceedings of the National Academy of Sciences* v.103/25 (2006), pp. 9381–9386.

[9]   (i) Marion Kim, "Catholics Accept Evolution Guided by God," *The Christian Post*, July 19, 2005.
      (ii) Richard Owen, "Vatican says Evolution does not prove the non-existence of God," *Times Online*, March 6, 2009.

[10] George Musser, "Could Time End?" *Scientific American* 303(3), September 2010, pp. 84–91.

[11] Ibid.

[12] Eliezer Zeiger, "Time, Space and Consciousness." BOr HaTorah Vol. 15, ed. Prof. Herman Branover (Israel: SHAMIR, 2005).

[13] "For a thousand years in your sight are but like yesterday when it is past" (Psalm 90:4) as interpreted in the Babylonian Talmud, Sanhedrin 97a and 97b.

[14] Vlatko Vedral, "Living in a Quantum World," *Scientific American*, June 2011, pp. 38–43.

[15] Avi Rabinowitz and Herman Branover, "The Role of the Observer in Halakhah and Quantum Physics," eds. H. Branover and I. Attia, (Northvale, NJ: *Science in the Light of the Torah: A B'or Ha'Torah Reader*, 1994).

[16] Kaufmann Kohler, M. Seligsohn, Isaac ben Samuel of Acre, 2002, JewishEncyclopedia.com.

[17] Rabbi Aryeh Kaplan, *The Age of the Universe: A Torah True Perspective* (Rueven Meir Caplan, 2008).

[18] Genesis 1:28.

Chapter 2

Divergent Views:
The Origins Debate

The creation–evolution controversy[1] (or the origins debate) is a recurring cultural, political, and theological dispute about the origins of the universe, earth, life, and humanity. The dispute continues between those who espouse religious belief and thus support a creationist view, and those who accept evolution as supported by scientific consensus. The dispute particularly involves the field of evolutionary biology, in addition to fields such as geology, paleontology, and cosmology.

Scientific Inquiry

Beginnings

Scientific inquiry began with the ancient Greeks. Although many Greeks retained religious beliefs about nature, some Greek philosophers proposed theories about the physical world based on reason. Questions revolving around the role of science in our origins reached a zenith during the Renaissance (a cultural movement that spanned the period roughly from the 14th to the 17th century), when science assumed a dominant role in cultural and educational forums. As science advanced, religious authority, particularly that of the Catholic Church, began to wane. Great thinkers and religious minds enlarged their vision of the universe to encompass a longer time span from the beginning of time to the current era. As religious authority dwindled during the 1700s, natural philosophers struggled even more insistently to devise purely material explanations for life.

An Old Earth

Around 1800, British civil engineer William Smith began documenting, for the first time, dramatic differences in the fossils found within specific layers of rock strata. Each era of rock formation appeared to have its own unique population of creatures. These discoveries in geology led to various theories of an ancient earth, and fossils revealing past extinctions prompted realization of evolutionary possibilities.

Evolution

As early as the late 1700s, the widespread acceptance of Pierre Simon Laplace's nebular hypothesis (a model explaining the formation and evolution of the solar system) established an evolutionary view of cosmic origins. The idea of organic evolution was widely disseminated by the early 1800s.

In 1858, after learning that naturalist Alfred Wallace had independently hit on the same idea, Charles Darwin, who had been working on his own ideas regarding natural selection for many years, finally announced his full-fledged theory and published *On the Origin of Species* in 1859. This book revolutionized biological thought.

On the Origin of Species launched an ongoing revolution in human thought. In the book, Darwin does not prove his theory of evolution by natural selection. Rather, he argues that it is a better explanation for the origin of organic species[2] than creationism. The implications of Darwin's theory provoked immediate controversy. Although accepting his theory did not preclude a belief in God, it did allow proponents to dispense with the need to believe in a supernatural creator of species or a literal interpretation of the Genesis creation account. Further, it undermined natural theology (man as a special creation) by suggesting that species evolve through random chance and a struggle for survival. Crucially, the theory required billions of years for species to evolve, not just six days.

From that point, the idea of evolution gained ascendancy in Western biology. It offered a plausible explanation for the origin of all species and raised a host of new issues for scientific study. By 1875, virtually all biologists in Europe and America had adopted an evolutionary view of origins.

Even as biologists accepted the basic theory of evolution, they came to doubt the sufficiency of Darwin's notion that the evolutionary process proceeded through random inborn variations selected by a competitive struggle for survival. Alternative mechanisms for evolution were considered, although an enhanced version of Darwin's theory proved ultimately successful in the end.

By 1900 most Western biologists and intellectuals accepted some theory of evolution; however, popular and religious opposition lingered. Technical arguments that appealed to scientists failed to persuade the public, particularly when it came to the notion that humans had evolved from apes. The fossil record became a barrier to widespread acceptance of scientific ideas. Opponents decried the lack of fossils linking either major biological types (such as reptiles and mammals) or humans to their alleged simian ancestors. Deeply religious folk rejected all challenges to the literal Biblical account of a six-day creation.

Genetics

In the early 1900s even evolutionists were mired in doubt and disagreement. Biologists still believed that evolution had occurred, but there was no consensus on how it operated. All options seemed inadequate, especially classical Darwinism. Then, as often happens in science, answers came from an unexpected source—genetics.

By the 1940s, consensus emerged among biologists on how the evolutionary process worked. Evolution was a purely materialistic process[3] driven by the natural selection of random variation at the genetic level. This so-called neo-Darwinian synthesis was more fully Darwinian than Darwin's own conclusions. The breakthrough was largely conceptual; evolution, or at least the mechanism by which it operates, was and remains an unproven theory at the macroscopic level of species changing into other, very different species.

Human Evolution

The idea of ape-to-human evolution found its original spark in the 1700s. The European voyages of discovery had revealed the existence of chimpanzees, orangutans, and gibbons.

Anatomical comparisons soon suggested these animals were somehow connected with human beings. In his 1766 book, the Comte de Buffon stated an ape "is only an animal, but a very singular animal, which a man cannot view without returning to himself."[4] The fact that humans and apes share many anatomical traits encouraged later naturalists to think of the two as related by descent. As early as 1794, the philosopher Delisle de Sales commented that the apes "seem to form an intermediate line between animals and human beings."[5]

Jean-Baptiste Lamarck (1744–1829) seems to have been the first naturalist to propose publicly and explicitly that human beings had evolved from apes.[6] After Lamarck, naturalists took the idea of ape-to-human evolution more and more as a given. Nevertheless, in the *Origin of Species* (1859), Darwin makes no mention of human evolution.

Darwin's friend and advocate, Thomas Henry Huxley, in his 1863 book *Evidence as to Man's Place in Nature* summarized the many anatomical traits shared by humans and apes, and asserted that such evidence supported the hypothesis that humans and apes had evolved from a recent common ancestor. His was the first book devoted expressly to the topic of human evolution. Darwin weighed in on the topic of human evolution 12 years after publication of *On the Origin of Species* with the publication of *The Descent of Man*.

In the years since Darwin and Huxley, a wide variety of fossils from hominins have been unearthed. Scientists are now convinced that some of these hominins were intermediary evolutionary forms leading to humans.

Creationism

Decades of popular concern over the theory of evolution erupted during the 1920s into a movement by conservative American Protestants against teaching evolution in public schools. The movement was part of their larger effort to defend traditional beliefs and values against liberalism in the church and secularism in society. The movement met immediate opposition from religious liberals and a broad array of secularists. The battle was joined over the theory of evolution since both sides viewed it as central to religious liberalism and scientific secularism. The antagonism reached its public climax in 1925, when Tennessee's new law against teaching evolution was challenged by a schoolteacher named John Scopes. The ensuing court case helped turn the issue into a flashpoint for public controversy. The anti-evolution statute was upheld as constitutional. Other American states and school districts imposed similar measures against teaching evolution in public schools.

Scientific Creationism

In 1959, after the commemoration of the centennial of Darwin's *On the Origin of Species*, scientists hailed the triumph of a consensus theory of evolution. Scientists largely ignored the persistent anti-evolutionism that marked conservative Christianity in America, and assumed that it would decline. However, the Judeo–Christian religious sectors had drifted toward a more literal interpretation of the Bible as the Word of God: the six days of creation as literal 24-hour days, and humanity as a divine creation. Coupled with the rise of neo-Darwinism, this movement heightened tensions between traditional religious beliefs and modern scientific thought. Those tensions underlay the phenomenal impact of *The Genesis Flood,*[7] a book published in 1961 that argued scientific evidence supports the Biblical account of creation. Containing assertions unsupported by the scientific community, the book nonetheless spawned a movement known as scientific creationism.

Scientific creationism swept through America's conservative Protestant churches during the 1960s and 1970s, reviving belief that God had created the universe and all species in the past 10,000 years. Rather than simply opposing evolution theory, believers now offered an alternative view for inclusion in public education. With the rise of the Christian Right in American politics, creationists imposed this theory in many areas until 1987 when the U.S. Supreme Court overturned creationist instruction as violating the Constitutional separation of church and state. One by one, each curriculum teaching scientific creationism was struck down as unconstitutional, culminating in a 1987 U.S. Supreme Court ruling against Louisiana's Balanced Treatment Act. The Court ruled that no law was needed to teach scientific evidence for or against evolution; therefore, this law must have been passed to promote religion. These rulings ended the teaching of scientific creationism in public schools.

Among the fifteen percent of Americans who reject divine intervention as having a part in our origins, a purely neo-Darwinian struggle for survival among randomly mutating genes explains human origins. Others in this camp, such as paleontologist Stephen Jay Gould (who died in 2002 but whose influence remains strong), believe the neo-Darwinian synthesis needs refinement to account for evolution; they remain confident, however, that wholly materialistic mechanisms, yet to be discovered, can accomplish this.

Creationists counter that evolution remains unproved. They maintain that alternative ideas (or at least scientific objections to materialism) belong in the classroom. Even many Americans who reject scientific creationism agree that an intelligent designer should not automatically be ruled out as the source of life and individual species. In the United States, the debate over origins remains as intense as ever.

Theistic Evolution

Lost in the polarized conflict between materialistic evolution and special creation are those who accept that earthly species evolve while at the same time seeing a role for God in that process. Broadly speaking, this is theistic evolution.

Some Darwinists also believe that certain human traits, such as love and consciousness, were specially created in evolved hominins to form humans. The Catholic Church accepts this position.

Between theistic evolutionists and special creationists are self-identified progressive creationists. They believe that God intervened at various points in the geologic past to create the basic life forms, which then evolved into the various species we know today.

About half of all Americans do not accept any significant role for evolution in the generation of different kinds of plants and animals. At most, they accept the so-called micro-evolution of nearly similar species, such as Darwin's finches on the Galapagos Islands.

Intelligent Design

During the 1990s, a loosely organized group of Christian scholars advanced the idea that species are simply too complex to evolve. While eschewing Biblical arguments and chronologies, they saw species as the product of intelligent design. Some in this group stress that science should not *a priori* exclude supernatural causes for natural phenomena; gaps and abrupt appearances in the fossil record are best explained by special creation.

Current Situation

Nearly 150 years after the 1859 publication of Darwin's theory of evolution by natural selection, the book remains central to scientific and popular debate over organic origins. Scientists generally accept and endorse its applications. Many others see it as flawed.

The abrupt nature of the fossil record, in particular the Cambrian explosion that shows a sudden beginning to complex life in a very short period, and the existence of traits such as love and consciousness, remains to some explainable only by creationism.

The division is partly underscored by an inability to reconcile the stories on a common timeline; the scientific account via the fossil record as opposed to the Genesis account. The most controversial element pertains to the nature of humans: special creations versus smart animals. Many have abandoned the early six-epoch view of Genesis (now known as old earth creationism[8]) and moved toward an interpretation of a literal six days (now known as young earth creationism[9]), with humans as very recent divine creations. Scientists, on the other hand, maintain a strict view of evolution as having occurred during the course of billions of years, in particular with humans evolving over millions of years, with no room for God.

Today, the origins debate, which has historically been prominent in the United States, has spilled into other countries. In Europe, the Committee on Culture, Science and Education of the Parliamentary Assembly of the Council of Europe recently issued a report on the attempt by U.S.-inspired creationists to promote creationism in European schools. The report states:

> If we are not careful, creationism could become a threat to human rights which are a key concern of the Council of Europe.... The war on the theory of evolution and on its proponents most often originates in forms of religious extremism which are closely allied to extreme right-wing political movements.... [S]ome advocates of creationism are out to replace democracy by theocracy.[10]

In the Islamic world, the situation is mixed.[11] In Egypt, evolution is currently taught in schools. Saudi Arabia and Sudan have both banned the teaching of evolution. Scientific creationism has also been heavily promoted in Turkey and in immigrant Muslim communities in Western Europe. In Israel the debate also continues, as illustrated below in a 2010 newspaper report:

> The Education Ministry's chief scientist sparked a furor Saturday with remarks questioning the reliability of evolution: "If textbooks state explicitly that human

beings' origins are to be found with monkeys', I would want students to pursue and grapple with other opinions. There are many people who don't believe the evolutionary account is correct," he said.[12]

In the U.S., the general public remains divided over the origins debate. Surveys (see Table 2.1[13]) indicate that just under half the population believes that God specially created the first humans. About a third affirm that God guided evolution. About 15% accept the God-less theory of origins that dominates science.

Table 2.1 Creation vs. Evolution - Beliefs in America

Belief system	Creationist view	Theistic evolution	Evolution
Beliefs	God created man pretty much in his present form at one time within the last 10,000 years.	Man has developed over millions of years from less advanced forms of life, but God guided this process, including man's creation.	Man has developed over millions of years from less advanced forms of life. God had no part in this process.
1982–JUL	44%	38%	9%
1993–JUN	47%	35%	11%
1997–NOV	44%	39%	10%
1999–AUG	47%	40%	9%
2001–FEB	45%	37%	12%
2004–NOV	45%	38%	13%
2007–MAY	43%	38%	14%
2010–DEC	40%	38%	16%
2012–MAY	46%	32%	15%

[1]   Edward J. Larson, *The Theory of Evolution: A History of Controversy* (U.S.A.: The Teaching Company, 2002).

[2]   Charles Darwin, *On the Origin of Species* (Cambridge: Harvard University Press, 1964).

[3]   Materialistic process means causally dependent only upon physical processes.

[4]   Georges-Louis Leclerc (Comte de Buffon), *Histoire naturelle*, (Paris: de L'imprimerie de F. Dufart, 1766), vol 14, p.4.

[5]   Delisle de Sales, *Histoire philosophique du monde primitive* (Paris: L'an Illdela Republique, 1795).

[6]   Jean-Baptiste Lamarck, *Philosophie zoologique*, (Paris: de L'Imprimerie de Duminil-Lesueur, 1809).

[7]   John C. Whitcomb and Henry M. Morris, *The Genesis Flood* (NJ: Presbyterian and Reformed Publishing Co., 1961).

[8]   Old earth creationism (OEC) is an umbrella term for a number of creationism proponents. This worldview is typically more compatible with mainstream scientific thought on the issues of geology, cosmology, and the age of the earth, particularly in comparison to young earth creationism. Nevertheless, OEC adherents still generally take the accounts of creation in Genesis more literally (albeit accepting the six-epoch view) than those who abide by theistic evolution (also known as evolutionary creationism), in that OEC rejects the scientific consensus accepting evolution.

[9]   Young earth creationism is a form of creationism that asserts the heavens, earth, and all life were created by direct acts of God during a relatively short period, sometime between 5,700 and 10,000 years ago. Adherents believe that God created the earth in six 24-hour days, taking a literal interpretation of the Genesis creation narrative as a basis for their beliefs.

[10]   Council of Europe, Parliamentary Assembly, Resolution 1580 (2007), *The Dangers of Creationism in Education*, text adopted by the Assembly on 4 October 2007 (35th Sitting) (see Doc. 11375, report of the Committee on Culture, Science and Education, rapporteur: Mrs. Brasseur).

[11]   Stephen Jones, "In the Beginning: The Debate over Creation and Evolution, Once Most Conspicuous in America, is Fast Going Global," *The Economist*, 19 April 2007.

[12]   Or Kashti, Zafrir Rinat, "Scientists Irate after Top Education Official Questions Evolution," Haaretz.com, 29 December 2010.

[13]   (i) "Reading the Polls on Evolution and Creationism," Pew Research Center Pollwatch, September 28, 2005.

(ii) "Evolution, Creationism, Intelligent Design," Gallup, Inc., July 14, 2012. www.gallup.com/poll/21814/evolution-creationism-intelligent-design.aspx. The small difference between the total and 100% owes to "don't know" responses.

Chapter 3

The Science Answer

Has the scientific method produced a timeline for the appearance of Homo sapiens? Has science identified our relation to other species? Has it produced an accurate picture of our early history?

If so, how complete is that information?

Evolution is the scientific theory to explain the appearance of life on earth, including Homo sapiens. The fossil record documents the history of Homo sapiens from their first appearance until thousands of years ago. Fossils present a clear outline for the appearance of life over the past 3.5 billion years. This record is independent of any theory, such as evolution, because it simply documents the timing of fossils as they are discovered, categorized, and dated. In addition, we are able to study and date other remains, such as tools and ancient soils, to extract further clues about earlier beings, e.g., the food they ate. Finally, recent development of the science of genetics allows us to extract genetic evidence from skeletons or remains (less than 100,000 years old) and compare it to current species. More importantly, the mapping of the human genome (the entirety of an organism's hereditary information) and other genomes, such as that of the chimpanzee, gives us a window onto the biology and the behavior of past beings far beyond that provided by a basic skeleton.[1]

The purpose of this chapter is to examine what both the fossil record along with other buried remains and genetic evidence tell us about the appearance and history of Homo sapiens. The information in this chapter summarizes the current state of scientific knowledge (as of 2012), relying upon peer reviewed articles and books written by well-respected scientists.

The scientific method provides a robust way to measure things, such as the age of bones. Over time, the scientific method has proved conducive to correct results—as long as these results can be tested. The scientific method has consistently yielded outstandingly accurate and useful findings on which we rely, and in fact trust, in our lives every day. There is no reason to doubt the fundamental accuracy of the body of knowledge comprising the age and nature of the fossil record and DNA analysis, although refinements continue to emerge on a routine basis.

A comparison of the Genesis creation narrative to scientific findings cannot be made without first understanding that testable knowledge, developed using the scientific method, is, by and large, accurate.

The Fossil Record

What is the Fossil Record?

Fossils (from Latin *fossus*, literally "having been dug up") are the preserved remains or traces of animals, plants, and other organisms from the remote past. The accumulation of fossils, both discovered and undiscovered, and their placement in fossil-containing rock formations and sedimentary layers (strata) is known as the fossil record. The study of fossils across geological time, their formation, and the evolutionary relationships among them are key functions of paleontology.

The fossil record depicts life's history as it unfolded over the span of 3.5 billion years.

Evidence of Life Preserved in the Fossil Record

Fossils can be microscopic, such as single bacterial cells only one micrometer in diameter, or gigantic, like dinosaurs and trees many meters long and weighing several tons. A fossil normally contains only a portion of the deceased organism, usually the part that was partially mineralized during life, such as the bones and teeth of vertebrates or the protective external skeletons of invertebrates. Fossils also may consist of marks left behind by the organism while it was alive, such as a footprint or feces. These are called trace fossils.

Dating the Fossil Record

Since the early 1900s, absolute dating methods, such as radiometric dating (including potassium/argon, argon/argon, uranium series, and, for very recent fossils, carbon14 dating), have been used to verify the relative ages of fossils and to provide absolute ages for many fossils. Radiometric dating has shown that the earliest known fossils are more than 3.4 billion years old. Various dating methods continue in use today. Despite some variance in these methods, they offer evidence for a very old earth, a planet of approximately 4.6 billion years.

Radioactive dating compares the amount of a naturally occurring radioactive isotope and its decay products, making use of known decay rates. All ordinary matter combines chemical elements, each with its own atomic number, indicating the number of protons in the atomic nucleus. Additionally, elements may exist in different isotopes, with each differing in the number of neutrons in the nucleus. A particular isotope of an element is called a nuclide. Some nuclides are inherently unstable. Eventually, an atom of such a nuclide will spontaneously decay (i.e., radioactively decay) into a different nuclide.

While the exact time at which a particular nucleus decays is unpredictable, a collection of radioactive nuclide atoms decays at a rate described by a parameter known as the half-life, usually given in units of years. After one half-life has elapsed, half of the nuclide's atoms will have decayed into a daughter nuclide, or decay product. Often, the daughter nuclide is radioactive, leading to the formation of another daughter nuclide, and eventually to a stable (non-radioactive) daughter nuclide; each step in this chain-like process is characterized by a distinct half-life. Usually the half-life of interest in radiometric dating is the longest in the chain, which is the rate-limiting factor in the ultimate transformation of the radioactive nuclide into its stable daughter. Isotopic systems that have been used for radiometric dating have half-lives ranging from only about ten years (tritium) to many thousands of years (carbon 14), to a billion years (potassium-argon), and to even longer periods of time.

Can We Trust the Results of Radiometric Dating?

A nuclide's half-life depends on its nuclear properties; it is not affected by external factors such as temperature, pressure, chemicals, or magnetic or electric fields. Nuclear properties and, therefore, the half-life of nuclides have remained stable[2] as the earth has evolved and undergone volcanism and weathering (including the Flood described in Genesis). Given this stability in materials containing a radioactive nuclide, the proportion of original nuclide to its decay product(s) has changed in a predictable way owing to the effects of decay over time. In this manner the abundance of related nuclides can be used as a clock to measure time between the incorporation of the original nuclide(s) into a material and the present.

Thus, every bone that is buried and contains radioactive material contains its own nuclear clock. When we uncover a bone today, we can read its age. Similar methods help us keep time, in a basic sense with nuclear clocks, and as a component of advanced systems requiring precise time measurement, from GPS satellite technologies to military weaponry.

The Sequence of Life Revealed in the Fossil Record

By synthesizing the fossil record, classifying fossils, determining their age, and placing them in the context of the geologic scale, scientists have revealed the sequence of life on earth:

1. The fossil record begins with 3.5 to 3.0 billion-year-old rocks from Australia and South Africa, in which are preserved the remains of blue-green algae. In rocks more than a billion years old, only fossils of single-celled organisms are found. In rocks that are about 550 million years old, fossils of simple, multi-cellular animals can be identified. Approximately 530 million years ago (Ma) there was an explosion of life, followed by the gradual appearance of new animals—yet, each within relatively short and even abrupt time frames: fish with jaws 400 million years ago, amphibians 350 million years ago, reptiles 300 million years ago, mammals 230 million years ago, and birds 150 million years ago.[3]

2. Fossilization is rare. Scientists have unearthed only 250,000 fossil species. Given the vast number of species throughout history, this is a remarkably small fraction. Indeed, the millions of species alive today constitute approximately one percent of all species that have existed.

3. In some cases, the fossil record can be interpreted to show that certain organisms progressed systematically

over time, each version displaying what appears to be a modification over the earlier. In other cases, there are large gaps in the fossil record, and the developmental process for some organisms is not as clear. Often, organisms lead to a dead end.

4. Throughout geologic time, life was punctuated by distinct events. Large numbers of organisms appeared in a short time span, and periodic mass extinctions occurred, such as at the end of the Cretaceous Period, when a majority of species disappeared over a relatively short time period.[4]

Table 3.1 summarizes the timeline for the appearance of life on earth up to the emergence of hominins.

Table 3.1 Timeline for Appearance of Life on Earth[5]

Time	Fossil record event
3.5 BY ago	The oldest fossils of single-celled organisms date from this time.
2.4 BY ago	The great oxidation event occurs, when oxygen begins to build in the atmosphere.
2.2 BY ago	Fossil evidence emerges of complex celled organisms.
535 Ma	The Cambrian explosion begins, with many new body forms appearing.
500 Ma	Animals were exploring land at this time.
425 Ma	First primitive macroscopic plants appear on land.
400 Ma	Oldest known insect lives about this time.
397 Ma	First four-limbed animals emerge.
310 Ma	Fossil forebears of all modern reptiles, dinosaurs, and birds have appeared.
215 Ma	First mammals appear.
150 Ma	First bird lives in Europe.
130 Ma	First flowering plants emerge.

Time	Fossil record event
65 Ma	The Cretaceous-Tertiary (K/T) extinction wipes out several species, including dinosaurs.
63 Ma	Primates split into two groups: dry-nosed primates and wet-nosed primates.
40 Ma	New World monkeys diverge from higher primates.
25 Ma	Apes split from Old World monkeys.
6–8 Ma	Hominins appear.

BY = billion years / Ma = million years ago

Information about Humans from Buried Remains

Humans leave behind much more than traditional fossils, for example, the cave paintings of Lascaux and other sites. Thus, a richer study of human origin and history can be made by considering not just the fossil record, but also other buried remains. Initially, paleoanthropologists studied how the human skeleton compared to other primates and ancient fossil remains. Then archaeologists studied how the stones and animal bones left by ancient people might relate to their behavioral patterns. Today, we also look at microscopic features of bone, teeth, and ancient soils that preserve evidence of ancient foods, growth rates, and cultural practices.[6]

Despite the rich knowledge obtained thus far, it must be understood that the fossil record of man and apes is very sparse. Approximately 95 percent of all known fossils are marine invertebrates, about 4.7 percent are algae and plants, about 0.2 percent are insects and other invertebrates, and only about 0.1 percent is vertebrates (animals with bones). Finally, only the smallest imaginable fraction of vertebrate fossils consists of primates (humans, apes, monkeys, and lemurs).[7]

Genetics

Recently, genetics has made a major contribution to understanding our origins and expansion across the globe.[8]

The human body is made of 50 to 100 trillion cells, which comprise the basic units of life and combine to form more complex tissues and organs. Inside each cell, genes form a blueprint for protein production that determines how the cell will function. Genes also determine physical characteristics, or traits. The complete set of some 20,000 to 25,000 genes is called the genome. Only a tiny fraction of the total genome sets the human body apart from that of animals.

Most cells have a similar structure. An outer layer, called the cell membrane, contains a gel-like substance called cytoplasm. Within the cytoplasm are many different specialized "little organs," called organelles. The most important of these is the nucleus, which controls the cell and houses the genetic material in structures called chromosomes. Another type is the mitochondria, which have their own genome and do not recombine during reproduction.

Chromosomes carry hereditary, genetic information in long strings of DNA (deoxyribonucleic acid) called genes. Humans have 22 numbered pairs of chromosomes and a single pair of sex chromosomes (XX in females and XY in males). Each chromosomal pair includes one inherited from the father and one from the mother.

DNA is the set of genetic instructions for creating an organism. Genes determine which proteins individual cells manufacture, and thus, which function particular cells will perform.

Mutations are random changes in an individual's DNA sequence that occur rarely in each new generation. They manifest during reproduction when particular DNA strands replicate themselves for the next generation, but not always perfectly. In this manner, genetic markers (a variation that leads to an observed trait) are inherited and passed down through the generations.

Y chromosome DNA, passed from father to son, and mitochondrial DNA, passed from mother to daughter, both occasionally experience mutations leading to markers. These mutations occurring in otherwise continuous genetic replication serve as signposts as part of the historical record of humans on earth. By following a marker back through time, geneticists identify the most recent common ancestor of all who have a particular marker. This way a full family tree of humans can be built and traced back to a common ancestor.

Thus, the study of genetics whereby genes of current human populations are compared to each other, to previous remains or fossil samples[9] and to the rest of the primates, further informs what we learn from the fossil record and other buried remains. This process of combining DNA and physical evidence to reveal the history of ancient humanity constitutes the emerging field of genetic anthropology. Genetics provides key information on how genetically similar or dissimilar we are to different primates, to prior hominids, and to each other.

In particular, genetics has helped to establish our single common ancestry in Africa and allowed us to trace our travels throughout the planet.

Much of this advance has been made possible by the scientific endeavors that aim to determine the complete genome sequence of humans and chimpanzees; the endeavors are known as genome projects.

The Genome Projects

Completed in 2003, the Human Genome Project[10] (HGP) was a 13-year project coordinated by the U.S. Department of Energy and the National Institutes of Health. The UK, Japan,

France, Germany, China, and other nations contributed to the project. Goals included identification of all the approximately 20,000 to 25,000 genes in human DNA, determination of the sequences of the 3 billion chemical base pairs that make up human DNA, and storage of the information in databases accessible to research and industry.

In early 2002, the National Human Genome Research Institute (NHGRI) agreed to support an initial chimpanzee genome sequencing project, which was expanded to include a higher quality gene sequencing objective in late 2003.

Significant information has been obtained from these projects and other studies. This information is usually quoted in a percentage of difference or similarity in genes. However, percentages can be calculated in varying ways and thus differ. Nonetheless, for any particular method of calculation, relative similarities and differences can be ascertained. For example,[11] the genetic difference between individual humans today is estimated at about 0.1% on average; study of the same aspects of the chimpanzee genome indicates a difference of about 1.2% (or 2% measured in a different manner).[12] The bonobo, which is a close cousin of chimpanzees, differs from humans to the same degree. The DNA difference with gorillas, another of the African apes, is about 1.6%. Most importantly, chimpanzees, bonobos, *and* humans all show this same amount of difference from gorillas. A difference of 3.1% distinguishes us and the African apes from the Asian great ape, the orangutan. The great apes and humans differ from rhesus monkeys, for example, by about 7% in their DNA.

Human Timeline

Scientists synthesize observable characteristics or traits of humans and their precursors, these including morphology, genetics, development, biochemical or physiological properties, behavior, and products of behavior (cave paintings and the like), to arrive at the timeline for the appearance of humans. The timeline encompasses the development of the genus Homo, including the emergence of Homo sapiens as a distinct species and a unique category of hominids and mammals.

The term "human" in the context of human evolution refers to the genus Homo, but studies of human evolution usually include other earlier hominins, such as the Australopithecines (a species that was bipedal and dentally similar to humans but with a brain size not much larger than that of modern apes), from which the genus Homo is thought to have diverged about 2.3 to 2.4 million years ago in Africa.[13]

The billions of human beings living today all belong to one species: Homo sapiens. As in all species, there is variation among individual human beings, from size and shape to skin tone and eye color. But we are much more alike than we are different. We are, in fact, remarkably similar. The DNA of all human beings living today is 99.9% alike.[14]

Overview

Humans are primates. Physical and genetic similarities show that the modern human species, Homo sapiens, has a very close relationship to another group of primate species, the apes. Hominins and the great apes (large apes) of Africa, chimpanzees and gorillas, are believed to share a common ancestor that lived between 8 and 6 million years ago.[15] Hominins first appeared in Africa. The fossils of early hominins who lived between 6 and 2 million years ago come entirely from Africa.

Most scientists currently recognize some 15 to 20 different species of hominins. Scientists do not all agree, however, about how these species are related, or which ones simply died out. In particular, several species and subspecies of Homo existed and are now extinct; examples include Homo erectus (which inhabited Asia, Africa, and Europe), and Neanderthals (which inhabited Europe and Asia). Archaic Homo sapiens appeared between 400,000 and 250,000 years ago.

The dominant view among scientists concerning the origin of anatomically modern humans, Homo sapiens, is the hypothesis known as Out of Africa, or recent African origin hypothesis,[16] which argues that Homo sapiens arose in Africa about 200,000 years ago[17] and had developed modern behaviors and migrated out of the continent by around 60,000 years ago. They then went on to replace populations of Homo erectus in Asia and Neanderthals in Europe, with the last of the other homo species (Neanderthals) becoming extinct about 30,000 years ago.

Modern Behaviors

Behavioral modernity[18] is a term used to refer to a set of traits that distinguish present-day humans and their recent ancestors from both living primates and other extinct hominid lineages. It is the point at which Homo sapiens began to demonstrate a reliance on symbolic thought and to express cultural creativity. Modern human behavior[19] is characterized by:

1. Abstract thinking: the ability to act with reference to abstract concepts not limited in time or space.

2. Planning depth: the ability to formulate strategies based on past experience and to act upon them in a group context.

3. Symbolic behavior: the ability to represent objects, people, and abstract concepts with arbitrary symbols, vocal or visual, and to reify such symbols in cultural practice.

4. Behavioral, economic and technological innovativeness.

Furthermore these developments are thought to be associated with the origin of language.[20]

The onset of modernity is not easy to define. Is it when humans first made sophisticated tools? When they first made elaborate cave paintings? When they first made jewelry for decoration or self-ornamentation? The debate continues.

The archaeological evidence available leaves little indication that Homo sapiens behaved any differently from earlier Homo until at least 120,000 years ago (or 120 KYA where KYA means one thousand years ago). They retained the same stone tools and hunted less efficiently than did modern humans. It is hard to date when modernity began, although most agree that the full set of modern behaviors had appeared by 60,000 years ago.

There are two main theories regarding the emergence of modern human behavior.[21] One theory holds that behavioral modernity occurred as a sudden event about 60,000 years ago. The second theory suggests that there was never any single technological or cognitive revolution. Proponents of this view argue that modern human behavior developed gradually. They point to arguably modern behaviors, such as use of pigment, decorations,[22] and burial of the dead, as far back as about 100,000 years ago. However, these early examples are only a few of the full set of key modern behaviors that had appeared by 60,000 years ago.

Out of Africa Migration

The migration of humans out of Africa to the entire world is a remarkable account reconstructed from buried remains and genetic analysis. It is not known why humans left Africa after being there for over 100,000 years, and why they felt compelled to inhabit every part of the world. However, various studies and simulations have revealed that climate change was a significant factor.[23] Climate affects food supply and human migration patterns match reasonably well with the availability of food. Furthermore, major climate change events facilitated the worldwide expansion. For example, the migration to Australia was facilitated by an ice age that lowered the sea level—making the island hopping journey from Asia to Australia possible.

Despite the role that climate change may have played in aiding the migration, what it took to accomplish the task was remarkable.[24] Migration required the rapid development of a vast range of new knowledge, tools and social arrangements. In Africa, people were tropical foragers. When humans moved toward northern Eurasia, they experienced a hostile climate where temperatures fell to -20°C for months at a time and there were often high winds. Surviving in such environments required tailored clothing, well-engineered shelters, and techniques for creating light and heat. Other travels and environments presented different problems. For example, much of the Americas were conquered by humans traveling in small water crafts, segment by segment, along the west coast. No small task—and still difficult today even with modern kayaks, VHF radios (to obtain regular weather and marine forecasts), and GPS!

Figure 3.1 shows a summary of the migrations.[25] Not shown are many smaller migrations, for example those to the interior of continents culminating with migrations into northern Canada and Europe, as well as the Sahara, by about 8,000 years ago.

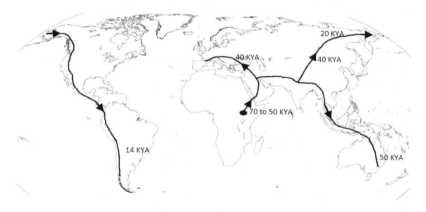

Figure 3.1 Summary of Human Migrations

Summary of the Human Timeline

Table 3.2 shows a very brief summary of the timeline for the appearance of humans and their early history.

Table 3.2 Human Timeline[26]

Time	Appearance
6–8 Ma	Hominins.
4.4 Ma	Ardipithecus, a very early hominin, had a small brain measuring about 350 cm³. It lived largely in the forest and was likely bipedal, although its feet were adapted for grasping rather than walking long distances.
3.6 Ma	Australopithecus afarensis, compared to modern and extinct great apes, had canines and molars that were reduced although still relatively larger than those of modern humans. A. afarensis also had a relatively small brain size (~380–430 cm³).
2.5 Ma	First Homo: Homo habilis, compared to modern humans, was short with disproportionately long arms and a brain slightly less than half the size of our brain. First to use stone tools. Became extinct by 1.4 Ma.

Time	Appearance
1.8 Ma	Homo erectus bore a striking resemblance to modern humans, but with a brain about 74% of modern size. Its forehead was less sloping and teeth were smaller. Lived side by side with Homo habilis until 1.4 Ma and became extinct by 400 KYA.
1.3 Ma	Homo in Europe.
200 KYA	Neanderthals, compared to humans, had more robust build and distinctive morphological features; were likely much stronger. Made advanced tools. Extinct by 30 KYA.
200 KYA	Homo sapiens, anatomically modern humans.
By 60 KYA	Behaviorally modern humans had appeared and left Africa.
60 KYA	Migration to South Asia.
50 KYA	Migration to Australia and Europe.
14 KYA	Migration to Americas, reaching southern Chile.
10 KYA	Evidence of farming and domestication of animals.

Human Speech and Language

Language is an important and unique aspect of human behavior. It is still unknown how and when language emerged.

Language is a very distinct and complex form of communication. Unlike visual communication, where one grasps a full picture at once, language is a form of communication that is serial. Language has to follow a specific order and requires great coordination. People make sounds using the vocal tract, throat, and mouth. Those sounds are transmitted to a listener, who hears them with his ears and then processes them with his brain. Not only is special equipment required to produce sound and to hear it, but also great intelligence is required to structure the communication resulting from sounds while maintaining full coordination with the breathing process. This is akin to playing music on an instrument. Not only is a musical instrument required, but one must also possess the intelligence and skill to work the instrument to produce the music.

For example, chimpanzees and bonobos don't have the vocal channel that humans do and therefore can't produce human speech sounds. However, they can learn how to make signs, and for this reason could be expected to communicate via sign language. Nonetheless, they simply do not possess the intelligence required to do so. Scientists[27] have taught a chimp, Kanzi, hundreds of signs. However, Kanzi has never mastered the combination of signs into longer utterances, something humans can manage by age two or three. Compared to humans, there seems to be a difference in chimpanzees' ability to generate this higher level of structure known as grammar.

The fossil record contains scant evidence of language development because it preserves very little about the structure of the brain and, in particular, the structure of the brain areas that may be related to language. Nonetheless, through genetic analysis and fossil remains, one can attempt to determine when the equipment to make and receive human language sounds emerged.

It is mostly undisputed that Australopithecines did not have communication systems significantly different from those found in great apes in general. Anatomical features such as the L-shaped vocal tract have appeared gradually in an evolving fashion, as opposed to appearing suddenly.[28] Hence it is most likely that Homo habilis and Homo erectus had some form of communication intermediate between that of modern humans and that of other primates.[29] Hominins who lived earlier than 300,000 years ago had a cranial nerve leading to the tongue (which is believed to reflect speech abilities) more akin to those of chimpanzees than modern humans.[30]

In 2007, the discovery of a Neanderthal with a modern-looking hyoid bone (or lingual bone, a horseshoe-shaped bone situated in the neck that serves as an anchoring structure for the larynx and is critical for speech production) suggests to some that Neanderthals may have been anatomically capable of producing sounds similar to modern humans.[31] However, many researchers conclude that the presence of this modern lingual bone is not sufficient to establish that the species was anatomically capable of making modern language sounds.[32]

In addition, even if Neanderthals may have been anatomically able to speak, scholars doubt that they possessed a fully modern language.[33] Neanderthals behaved the same as earlier hominin populations that did not have language apparatus; had Neanderthals possessed a fully modern language capability we would expect them to have behaved more like modern humans. As we have seen with Kanzi, the key to our complex form of communication is not equipment, but rather the ability to structure communication via grammar.

Grammar has always been the central focus of linguistics. One of the most famous figures in the study of grammar is the linguist Noam Chomsky. He argues[34] there are patterns that occur in human languages that cannot be learned by simply listening to what other people say. Humans seem to be born with an innate ability to sift out patterns that aren't obvious from the speech around them so they can create those patterns. Chomsky calls this argument the poverty of the stimulus—the stimuli that are present in an environment aren't enough to master a natural language.

Today's linguists disagree with Chomsky about the extent to which language is innate.[35] Many believe that language is largely learned uniquely and differently by different kinds of people. However, a recent finding obtained by research with infants suggests that the neural foundations of language acquisition are present at birth.[36] In summary, there is scientific consensus that language is unique to our species, and there is evidence that suggests that language could be innate. Finally, as is the case with the emergence of modern human behaviors, there is no agreement on the exact time when language emerged, although most believe it evolved concurrently with modern human behavior.

---

[1]   John Hawks, *The Rise Of Humans: Great Scientific Debates*, (U.S.A. The Teaching Company, 2011), Introduction.

[2]   G.T. Emery, "Perturbation of Nuclear Decay Rates," *Annual Review of Nuclear Science* (ACS Publications) v. 22, 1972, pp. 165–202. Note that the most reliable dating involves the use and overlap of several radioactive isotope series.

[3]   Michael Marshall, "Timeline: The Evolution of Life," *New Scientist*, 14 July 2009.

[4]   Stephen Jay Gould, "The Evolution of Life on Earth," *Scientific American*, October 1994, pp. 85–91.

[5]   (i) Michael Marshall, "Timeline: The Evolution of Life," *New Scientist*, 14 July 2009.

(ii) Stephen Jay Gould, *The Book of Life: An Illustrated History of the Evolution of Life on Earth*, Second Edition (New York: W. W. Norton Inc., 2001).

(iii) David M. Raup and J. John Sepkoski Jr., "Mass Extinctions in the Marine Fossil Record," *Science* v. 215 No. 4539, 19 March 1982, pp. 1501–1503.

(iv) John Alroy, "Dynamics of Origination and Extinction in the Marine Fossil Record," *The National Academy of Sciences of the USA*, 105 Supplement 1 (2008 August 12), pp. 11536–11542.

[6]   John Hawks, *The Rise Of Humans: Great Scientific Debates*, (U.S.A. The Teaching Company, 2011), Introduction.

[7]   "Facts on fossil record," Wisconsin Regional Primate Research Center, April 26 2001, Primate Info Net. www.primate.wisc.edu/pin/askfaq.html.

[8]   (i)Chris Johns (Editor) "The Greatest Journey Ever Told: The Trail of Our DNA," *National Geographic*, Vol. 209, No. 3, March 2006.

(ii) Noah A. Rosenberg, et al, "Genetic Structure of Human Populations," *Science*, v. 298 no. 5602, (20 December 2002), pp. 2381–2385.

(iii) Mark Stoneking and Johannes Krause, "Learning about human population history from ancient and modern genomes," *Nature Reviews Genetics*, 12, September 2011, pp. 603–614.

[9]   DNA fragments can survive for 50,000 to 100,000 years.

[10]   U.S. Department of Energy Genome Programs, genomics.energy.gov.

[11]   Mark Stoneking and Johannes Krause, "Learning about human population history from ancient and modern genomes," *Nature Reviews Genetics*, 12, September 2011, pp. 603–614.

[12]   The Chimpanzee Sequencing and Analysis Consortium, "Initial sequence of the chimpanzee genome and comparison with the human genome," *Nature*, 437, 1 September 2005, pp. 69–87.

[13]   John Hawks, *The Rise Of Humans: Great Scientific Debates*, (U.S.A. The Teaching Company, 2011), p. 3.

[14]   Noah A. Rosenberg, et al, "Genetic Structure of Human Populations," *Science*, v. 298 no. 5602, (20 December 2002), pp. 2381–2385.

[15]   (i) John Hawks, *The Rise Of Humans: Great Scientific Debates*, (U.S.A. The Teaching Company, 2011). The time of the first common ancestor maybe revised to as much as a few million years earlier, although current consensus is still 6–8 million years ago. See Catherine Brahic, "Our true dawn," *New Scientist*, v. 16, No 2892, (November 24, 2012) pp. 34–37.

(ii) Katherine Harmon, "Shattered Ancestry" *Scientific American* 308(2), February 2013, pp. 42–49.

[16] Paul Mellars, "Why Did Modern Human Populations Disperse from Africa ca. 60,000 Years Ago?" *Proceedings of the National Academy of Sciences*, v.103/25 (2006), pp. 9381–9386.

[17] The earliest fossil evidence comes from skulls dated at 195,000 years ago. See Michael Hopkin, "Ethiopia is top choice for cradle of Homo sapiens," *Nature News* (2005–02–16), doi:10.1038/news050214–10.

[18] Kate Wong, "The Morning of the Modern Mind," *Scientific American*, July 2005, No. 23, pp. 12–19.

[19] Sally McBrearty, Alison S Brooks, "The Revolution That Wasn't: A New Interpretation of the Origin of Modern Human Behavior" *Journal of Human Evolution*, 39, 2000. pp.453–563.

[20] Paul Mellars, "Why Did Modern Human Populations Disperse from Africa ca. 60,000 Years Ago?" *Proceedings of the National Academy of Sciences*, v.103/25 (2006), pp. 9381–9386.

[21] Hillary Mayell, "When Did 'Modern' Behavior Emerge in Humans?" *National Geographic News*, February 20, 2003. news.nationalgeographic.com/news/2003/02/0220_030220_h umanorigins2.html.

[22] Abdeljalil Bouzouggar, et al, "82,000-year-old shell beads from North Africa and implications for the origins of modern human behavior," *Proceedings of the National Academey of Sciences USA*, 104(24), 2007 June 12, pp. 9964–9.

[23] (i) Mati Milstein, "Climate Change Allowed Humans to Migrate Out of Africa", *National Geographic Adventure*, August 29 2007, http://news.nationalgeographic.com/news/2007 /08/070829-africa-rains_2.html.

(ii) Robert Marshall, "Climate change key to world domination", *New Scientist*, Vol. 215, No. 2883, September 22 2012, p. 12.

[24] Robert Boyd, et al, "The cultural niche: Why social learning is essential for human adaptation," *PNAS*, v. 108 no. Supplement 2 June 28, 2011, pp. 10918–10925.

[25] (i) Chris Johns (Editor) "The Greatest Journey Ever Told: The Trail of Our DNA," *National Geographic*, Vol. 209, No. 3, March 2006.

(ii) Heather Pringle, "The 1st Americans," *Scientific American*, November 2011, pp. 36–45.

[26] John Hawks, *The Rise Of Humans: Great Scientific Debates*, (U.S.A. The Teaching Company, 2011).

[27] John Hawks, *The Rise Of Humans: Great Scientific Debates*, (U.S.A. The Teaching Company, 2011), p. 93.

[28] Steve Olson, *Mapping Human History* (Boston: Houghton Mifflin Books, 2002). "Any adaptations produced by evolution are useful only in the present, not in some vaguely defined future. So the vocal anatomy and neural circuits needed for language could not have arisen for something that did not yet exist."

[29] Merritt Ruhlen, *Origin of Language* (NY: Wiley, 1994). p. 3 "Earlier human ancestors, such as Homo habilis and Homo erectus, would likely have possessed less developed forms of language, forms intermediate between the rudimentary communicative systems of, say, chimpanzees and modern human languages."

[30] B. Arensburg, A. M. B. Vandermeersch, H. Duday, L. A. Schepartz and Y. Rak, "A Middle Palaeolithic human hyoid bone," *Nature* 338, 1989, pp. 758–760.

[31] B. Arsenburg, et al., "A reappraisal of the anatomical basis for speech in middle Palaeolithic hominids," *American Journal of Physiological Anthropology* 83, 1990, pp. 137–146.

[32] Tecumseh W. Fitch, "The evolution of speech: a comparative review," *Trends in Cognitive Science*, Vol. 4, No. 7, July 2000, pp. 258–266.

[33] (i) Erica Klarreich, "Biography of Richard G. Klein." *Proceedings of the National Academy of Sciences of the United States of America* 101 (16), April 20, 2004, pp. 5705–5707.

(ii) Richard G. Klein, "Three Distinct Human Populations," *Biological and Behavioral Origins of Modern Humans.* Access Excellence @ The National Health Museum. Retrieved 2011–12–28, www.accessexcellence.org/BF/bf02/klein/bf02e3.php.

(iii) David Robson, "Puzzles of evolution: When did language evolve?," *New Scientist* 2857, March 24, 2012, p. 38.

34   John Hawks, *The Rise Of Humans: Great Scientific Debates,* (U.S.A. The Teaching Company, 2011), p. 93.

35   John Hawks, *The Rise Of Humans: Great Scientific Debates,* (U.S.A. The Teaching Company, 2011), pp. 94–95.

36   Judit Gervain, Iris Berent, and Janet F. Werker, "Binding at Birth: The Newborn Brain Detects Identity Relations and Sequential Position in Speech," *Journal of Cognitive Neuroscience,* Vol. 24, No. 3, March 2012, pp. 564–574.

Chapter 4

Interpreting Scriptures

Many people read the Bible generally, and Genesis in particular, as a mythological account of human origins. Others take the Bible's account quite literally.

Is it possible that Genesis contains a reliable timeline of key events related to the advent of humans? If so, how complete is that information, and how does it compare to today's scientific observations?

As we have seen in Chapter 1 of this book, Genesis is not intended to be a science text. However, given that it is part of the Torah, and the Torah provides a blueprint for creation, it must represent an accurate description of events and their timing. The entire creation account in Genesis Chapter 1 through Chapter 3 totals a mere 2,000 words or so, while the historical account of early Biblical characters in Chapters 4 through Chapter 11 is but approximately 5,000 words, not much longer than most introductory chapters of books on evolution. Can the Torah then possibly contain a detailed timeline of such rich meaning in so few words? And, where can we find the formula to convert the creation timeline to the time of events as measured by scientists (Human Time)?

Fortunately, the Torah consists of both the Written Law and the Oral Law. The brief account of our origins in the Written Law, as detailed in Genesis, is elaborated on significantly in the Oral Law. This oral tradition, together with related commentaries and mystical works, rivals, even when confined to the creation account only, the combined length of many contemporary biology books.

In fact, the Torah offers in-depth descriptions of what has happened since the beginning of time, specifying when and why it happened; in particular, pertaining to the creation of humans. This constitutes the Genesis timeline for the appearance of humanity and our early history.

The purpose of this chapter is to briefly summarize the method used to extract information from Genesis, to examine the sources that help us do so, and to look at key characters behind some of these sources.

The following is not an exhaustive review of this very complex subject; rather, the material is meant to provide an abbreviated understanding of the sources used throughout the rest of the book to arrive at a comparison of the creation narrative with scientific theory and observation. It also is intended to inspire admiration for the richness of Biblical sources.

This chapter likewise does not describe the Biblical answer regarding a timeline for the appearance and early history of humanity (unlike Chapter 3, which describes the science-based answer). The Biblical answer is developed in later chapters, as required to form a comparison with science's answer.

The rest of the book includes many references to Biblical topics; these are found primarily in sources described in this chapter.

Genesis as a Valuable Information Source

The Biblical Hebrew language is unlike any other language. While its pictograph letters are not unique, that each letter represents both a letter and a number does set it apart from other human communication systems. The numerical value of a letter, and therefore the word or sentence made from letters, contains meaningful information that has become a focus of study regarding mystical aspects of the oral tradition.

Hebrew is written from right to left. The shape of each letter contains deep significance and meaning while likewise correlating to a major field of study. For example, the first letter in the alphabet, Alef א, has a form that represents the way man was created: *"in our image after our likeness."*[1] The name for the first man, Adam, is a compound of "a" alef (its first letter), corresponding in Hebrew to *"our image,"* and dam (the next two letters), corresponding to *"after our likeness."* The shape of the letter consists of two small stubs, one on the upper right and one on the lower left, representing heaven and earth (or God and man's soul), with a diagonal line separating and uniting them simultaneously. This is the secret of the image in which man was created, meaning that he is partly on earth and partly in heaven. This will become much clearer in later chapters when we study humans. Alef numerically represents the number one. One is the only number that counts something (one) from nothing (zero); after that, all counting is something from something. The Alef is thus the beginning of the process in nature—it begins from nothing (i.e., created by God).[2] Elaborations on the meaning of the Alef's shape go on for pages in the literature.

Reading Hebrew text is akin to simultaneously reading English (letters and words), reading a scientific formula (e.g., a chemical or physics formula), and reading an abstract diagram explaining various connections and processes. In addition to this richness within the text, there is an oral tradition of divinely revealed text elaboration providing even more detail and helping to guide interpretation as well as connect various sections of the Bible, enabling one to glean even further information.

Needless to say, the process of reading Hebrew text to discern its full meaning requires years of study, an amazing memory and intellect, and teamwork—an effort not unlike developing a scientific theory.

Let us now look at the process and sources used in this book to arrive at the Human Time events described in Genesis.

How Is Genesis Used to Derive Human Time for Events Measured by Scientists?

Figure 4.1 illustrates the Biblical sources and how they are used in the book.

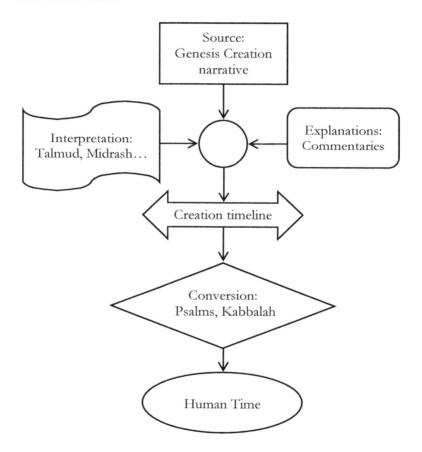

Figure 4.1 Biblical Sources

The process used to arrive at Human Time for events in the Genesis narrative is as follows:

1. We begin with the fundamental source—the Genesis creation narrative.

2. We use the oral tradition to interpret Genesis and to obtain a more exact time for each event.

3. We consult key commentaries for clarification and explanations of terms, events, and meaning.

4. Having arrived at an understanding of the events and the time at which they happen (in Creation Time), we convert from Creation Time to Human Time, using the mystical works.

Let us now review the sources and characters in each of these steps. (Genesis, the fundamental source, has been described already; at this point, a review of Annex A containing the Genesis creation text may be helpful.)

Interpretation: The Oral Tradition

Two key components of the Oral Law provide more exact times for each creation event and help us to chronologically organize events: the Talmud and some elements of Midrashim. These sources, along with the rest of the oral tradition, are thought to have been taught to Moses.[3] In fact, they are the reason why Moses remained so long on the mountain (as described in the Book of Exodus), as God could have given him the written law in one day. Moses is said to have transmitted this Oral Law to Joshua; Joshua, in turn transmitted it to the 70 Elders; the Elders to the Prophets; and the Prophets to the Great Synagogue.[4] It is believed the teachings were later transmitted successively to certain rabbis. Following the destruction of the Second Temple and the fall of

Jerusalem in 70 CE, it became apparent that the Hebrew community and its learning resources were threatened, and publication was the only way to ensure the Oral Law would be preserved. Thus, around 200 CE, a preserved version of the Oral Law in writing was completed.

The Talmud gets its name from the word *Lamud*, or "taught," meaning "the Teaching." The Mishnah is the foundation and principal part of the Talmud. It was expounded in the academies in Babylon and in Israel during the Middle Ages. In this book, all Talmudic references are from the Babylonian Talmud. As the interpretations increased with the passing of time, the disputations and decisions of the doctors of the law concerning the Mishnah were written down, and these writings constituted another part of the Talmud called the Gemarah. The Mishnah serves first as a kind of redaction of law, and is followed by the Gemarah, serving as an analysis of various opinions leading to definite decisions.

What kind of information does the Talmud reveal about timelines and creation? Below is an excerpt of the detailed timeline for the creation of man revealed for Day 6:

> *The day consisted of twelve hours. In the first hour, his [Adam's] dust was gathered; in the second [hour], it was kneaded into a shapeless mass. In the third [hour], his limbs were shaped; in the fourth...*[5]

Midrash means "exposition," and it denotes the non-legalistic teachings of the Rabbis of the Talmudic era. Midrash[6] designates a critical explanation or analysis which, going more deeply than the mere literal sense, attempts to penetrate into the spirit of the scriptures, to examine the text from all sides, and thereby to derive interpretations that are not immediately obvious.

In the centuries following the compilation of the Talmud (about 505 CE), much of this material was compiled into collections known as Midrashim. A prominent example of a Midrash used throughout this book is the Midrash Rabbah, which adds critical details to the Five Books of Moses; another example is Pirkê de Rabbi Eliezer, which includes the impacts on Adam and Eve resulting from their sin.

Table 4.1 provides a summary timeline of events and persons described in this chapter.

Table 4.1 Timeline of Biblical Sources and Persons

Time Biblical Year	Time Western calendar	Event or person
1	3760 BCE	Adam & Eve created
2448	1313 BCE	Torah received by Moses
	1st–2nd century	Author of Pirkê de Rabbi Eliezer
3979	219 CE	Mishna compiled
	3rd century	Author of Midrash Rabbah
4128	368 CE	Jerusalem Talmud compiled
4186	426 CE	Babylonian Talmud compiled
4260	500 CE	Babylonian Talmud recorded
4800–4865	1040–1105 CE	Rashi
4954–5030	1194–1270 CE	Ramban
	13th century	Zohar appears in Spain
	13th–14th centuries	Isaac ben Samuel of Acre
5294–5332	1534–1572 CE	Arizal

Midrash Rabbah

Midrash Rabbah[7] is dedicated to explaining the Five Books of Moses. Genesis Rabbah is a Midrash to Genesis, assigned by tradition to the renowned Jewish scholar of Palestine, Hoshaiah (circa third century), who commented on the teachings of the Oral Law. The Midrash forms a commentary on the whole of Genesis. The Biblical text is expounded verse for verse, often word for word; only genealogic passages and similar non-narrative information for exposition are omitted.

Midrash Rabbah contains many simple explanations of words and sentences, often in the Aramaic language, suitable for the instruction of youth; it also includes the most varied expositions popular in the public lectures of the synagogues and schools. According to the material or sources at the disposal of the Midrash's editor, he has strung together various longer or shorter explanations and interpretations of successive passages, sometimes anonymously, sometimes citing the author. He adds to the running commentary connected in some way with the verse in question, or with one of its explanations—a method not unusual in the Talmud and other Midrashim. The chapters of Genesis about the creation of the world and of humans in turn furnish remarkably rich material for this type of commentary. Entire sections are devoted to the discussion of one or two verses of Genesis.

What kind of information does Midrash Rabbah reveal about the early history of humankind? Many kinds, for example, it gives us surprisingly specific information about the Genesis Flood:

> The deluge in the time of Noah was by no means the only flood with which this earth was visited. The first flood did its work of destruction as far as Jaffé, and the one of Noah's days extended to Barbary.[8]

Barbary refers to the western coastal regions of North Africa, what are now Morocco, Algeria, Tunisia, and Libya.

Pirkê de Rabbi Eliezer

Pirkê de Rabbi Eliezer (or "Chapters of Rabbi Eliezer")[9] comprises ethical guidelines as well as significant information about Adam and Eve. Many details not found in other sources are revealed in this work.

Despite the book's bearing an author's name, the actual writer is unknown. The reputed author is Rabbi Eliezer, who lived in the latter half of the first century CE and in the first decades of the second century. He was famous for outstanding scholarship and is quoted in the Mishnah and Talmud more frequently than any of his contemporaries. Did this owe to the fact that the actual writer of Chapters of Rabbi Eliezer deliberately selected the name of this famous master in Israel as its alleged author? In many respects the book is controversial and unorthodox: controversial in opposing doctrines and traditions current in certain circles of former times; unorthodox in revealing mysteries (including creation mysteries) that were reputed to have been taught in the school of Rabban Jochanan ben Zakkai, the teacher of Rabbi Eliezer.

Who exactly was the teacher of Rabbi Eliezer? Rabban Jochanan ben Zakkai,[10] who flourished in the first century CE, helped to preserve and develop Judaism in the years following the destruction of the Second Temple of Jerusalem in 70 CE. He is said to have been smuggled out of the besieged city in a coffin, and to have visited the Roman camp and persuaded the future emperor Vespasian to allow him to set up an academy at Jabneh near the Judean coast. Jochanan established an authoritative rabbinic body there and was revered as a great teacher and scholar. According to the Mishnah,[11] traditions were handed down through an unbroken chain of scholars; Jochanan, in receiving the teachings of Hillel and Shammai, formed the last link in that chain. Before his death, Hillel is said to have prophetically designated Jochanan, his youngest pupil, as "the father of wisdom" and "the father of coming generations."

What did Rabbi Eliezer learn about Adam and Eve? For example, he tells us that as a result of her part in the sin, Eve (and all women) received the following curses: "*the afflictions arising from menstruation and the tokens of virginity; the affliction of conception in the womb; and the affliction of child-birth; and death.*"[12]

Explanations - The Commentaries

Commentaries are critical explanations or interpretations of the Biblical texts. The process of arriving at these explanations is rigorous and involves very specific and well-developed rules and methods for the investigation and exact determination of the meaning of the scriptures, both legal and historical.

The interpretation of the Biblical text examines its extended meaning. As a general rule, the extended meaning never contradicts the basic meaning. Commentaries explore four levels of meaning: (1) the plain or contextual meaning of the text, (2) the allegorical or symbolic meaning beyond the literal sense, (3) the metaphorical or comparative meaning as derived from similar occurrences in the text, and (4) the hidden or mystical meaning. There is often considerable overlap, for example when legal understandings of a verse are influenced by mystical interpretations, or when a hint is identified by comparing a word with other instances of the same word.

Two major commentaries used throughout this book are those by Rashi and Ramban. Rashi's commentary is widely known for presenting the plain meaning of the text in a concise yet lucid fashion. Ramban's commentary attempts to discover the hidden meanings of scriptural words.

Rashi

Shlomo Yitzhaki (1040–1105 CE), better known by the acronym Rashi[13] (RAbbi SHlomo Itzhaki), was a medieval French rabbi famed as being the author of the first comprehensive commentary on the Talmud, as well as for authoring a comprehensive commentary on the Written Law (including Genesis). His is considered the father of all commentaries that followed on the Talmud and the Written Law.

Rashi, acclaimed for his ability to present the basic meaning of the text succinctly, appeals to both learned scholars and beginning students. His works remain a centerpiece of contemporary study. Rashi's commentary on the Talmud, which covers nearly all of the Babylonian Talmud, has been included in every edition of the Talmud since its first printing in the 1520s. His commentary on the Five Books of Moses is an indispensable aid to students at all levels. The latter commentary alone serves as the basis for more than 300 super-commentaries that analyze Rashi's choice of language and citations.

Rashi began to write his famous commentary at an early age. Because the Torah was very difficult to properly understand, and the Talmud was even more challenging, Rashi decided to write a commentary in simple language that would allow everyone to more easily learn and understand the Torah. As Rashi was modest, and even after he had become famous far and wide, he hesitated to come out into the open with his commentary. He wanted to first make sure that it would be favorably received. So, he wrote his commentaries on slips of parchment and set out on a two-year journey, visiting the various Torah academies of those days. He traveled incognito, always hiding his identity.

Rashi came to a Torah academy and sat down to listen to the lecture of the attending rabbi. There came a difficult passage that the rabbi struggled to explain to his students. When Rashi was left alone, he took the slip with his commentary, in which that passage was explained simply and clearly, and put it into one of the rabbi's books. On the following morning when the rabbi opened his book, he found a mysterious slip of parchment in which the passage was so clearly and simply explained that he was amazed. He told his students about it. Rashi listened to their praises of his commentary and saw how useful it was to the students, but he did not say that it was his. And so Rashi went on visiting various academies of the Torah in many cities, and everywhere he planted his slips of commentaries secretly. The way these slips were received made Rashi realize more and more how useful they were, and he continued to write his commentaries. Finally, Rashi was discovered planting his commentary in the usual manner, and the secret was out.

What kind of information on the Creation narrative does Rashi reveal? One example is he teaches that when the Genesis text says, God made man "*after our likeness*," it means 'He made man with the power of understanding and intellect.'[14]

Ramban

Nachmanides, also known as Rabbi Moses ben Nachman Girondi, Bonastrucça Porta, and by his acronym Ramban[15] (Gerona, 1194–Land of Israel, 1270), was a leading medieval scholar, rabbi, philosopher, physician, and Biblical commentator. His commentary on the Five Books of Moses was his last and best known work. He is considered one of the elder sages of mystical Judaism. The Ramban's commentary on the Torah is believed to be based on careful scholarship and original study of the Bible.

Ramban showed great talent at a very early age. He was a brilliant student, and his scholarship, piety and fine character made him famous far beyond his own community. At the age of 16 he had mastered the whole Talmud with all its commentaries. Nachmanides also studied medicine and philosophy. Not wishing to profit from the Torah, Ramban became a practicing physician in his native town of Gerona, Spain. At the same time he was also the communal Rabbi of Gerona, and later became the Chief Rabbi of the entire province of Catalonia in Spain.

What information pertaining to the story of creation does Ramban reveal? As one example, he teaches that when the Genesis text says, God made man "*after our likeness*," it means 'He made man with moral freedom and free will.'[16]

Mystical Tradition

Kabbalah is the Jewish mystical tradition that teaches the deepest insights into the essence of God, His interaction with the world, and the purpose of Creation. This tradition provides insight into the nature of the human soul, and in particular, Adam's soul, and what happened to his soul as a result of the sin, to help us decipher the appearance of humans on earth.

The mystical tradition and its teachings—no less than the Oral Law—are an integral part of the oral tradition. They are traced back to God's revelation to Moses at Sinai, and some even before (one book is said to have been Adam's). The Zohar teaches[17] that science will inform spirituality, and spirituality will inform science by the time the Messianic era arrives. Kabbalah means 'reception,' for we cannot physically perceive the Divine; we merely study the mystical truths.

The primary mystical work is the Zohar.[18] The work is a revelation from God communicated through Rabbi Shimon bar Yochai to the latter's select disciples. Under the form of a commentary on the Five Books of Moses, written partly in Aramaic and partly in Hebrew, it contains a complete theosophy discussing the nature of God, the cosmogony and cosmology of the universe, the soul, sin, redemption, good, evil, and so on.

The Zohar first appeared in Spain in the 13th century and was published by Moses de Leon. De Leon ascribed the work to Shimon bar Yochai, a rabbi of the second century, who, during the Roman persecution, hid in a cave for 13 years studying the Torah and was divinely inspired to write the Zohar.

The father of contemporary Kabbalah is Rabbi Isaac Luria.

Rabbi Isaac Luria (Ari or Arizal)

Rabbi Isaac Luria (1534–1572) is commonly known as the Ari, an acronym standing for Elohi Rabbi Isaac, the Godly Rabbi Isaac. No other sage ever had 'Godly' as a preface to his name. This was a sign of what his contemporaries thought of him. To this day Rabbi Isaac Luria is referred to as Rabbenu HaAri, HaAri HaKadosh (the holy Ari) or Arizal (the Ari of blessed memory).

At a very early age, Rabbi Isaac Luria lost his father and he went to Cairo, Egypt, where an uncle took care of his upbringing and education. The brilliant youngster's studies of the Talmud promoted him to the heights of scholarly achievement. Yet Rabbi Isaac Luria's deep and introspective nature left him unsatisfied by the study of solely traditional sources. He acquired knowledge of Torah and devoted his entire life to its study and dissemination. At an early age he lived by himself for seven years, immersed in the study of the Zohar and other writings.

In his tireless efforts to penetrate the inner chambers of the Torah, he was able to work out an entire system of Kabbalistic doctrine on the world. About the year 1569, he took his family and migrated to Jerusalem, and from there to Safed (in northern Israel), the center of all study of the mystical tradition. Soon, a large group of disciples gathered about him.

Among the most ardent exponents of the Arizal's teachings was his disciple and successor, Rabbi Hayyim ben Joseph Vital. Rabbi Vital recorded the revelations and explanations of his great master. The Arizal died at the age of 38.[19]

The Arizal is considered the father of contemporary Kabbalah or Lurianic Kabbalah. His teachings describe new coherent doctrines of the origins of Creation and its cosmic rectification,[20] incorporating a recasting and fuller systemization of preceding teachings. In particular, the Arizal's extensive teachings on the subject of souls are contained in the book *Shaar HaGilgulim*, composed by Rabbi Hayyim ben Joseph Vital and his son Shmuel.[21]

Time Conversion—Mystical Works

The works described so far (along with a few others) develop an accurate Biblical representation of the appearance of humans in Creation Time. To convert from Creation Time to Human Time, a mystical source is required.

Among the many works, the ones discussed so far are mainstream. To convert timelines, we rely primarily on the eccentric and unconventional work of Isaac ben Samuel of Acre, *Otzar HaChaim*.

Isaac ben Samuel of Acre

Isaac ben Samuel of Acre[22] (fl. 13th–14th centuries) was a Kabbalist who lived in the land of Israel. It is thought Isaac ben Samuel was a pupil of Ramban. Isaac ben Samuel was at Acre when that town was taken by Al-Malik al-Ashraf, and he was thrown into prison with many fellow believers. Escaping the massacre in 1305, he went to Spain. This was the time that Moses de Leon discovered the Zohar.

According to Azulai,[23] Isaac ben Samuel of Acre is frequently quoted by prominent Kabbalists (e.g., Rabbi Hayyim ben Joseph Vital; Calabria, 1543–Damascus, 1620). He was an expert in composing the sacred names of God, by the power of which angels were forced to reveal to him the great mysteries. He wrote many works.

Rabbi Isaac ben Samuel developed an original methodology of interpretation, which he designated as the "four ways of NiSAN," being the acronym of Nistar (hidden), Sod (secret), Emet (truth), and Emet Nekhona (correct truth). The four ways of NiSAN are used by Rabbi Isaac ben Samuel only in his later works, including *Otzar HaChaim*. This work was translated to English recently by Rabbi Aryeh Kaplan, described in his own words as follows:[24]

> There is only one complete copy of this manuscript in the world, and this is in the Guenzberg Collection in the Lenin Library in Moscow.... This is how I got my hands on this very rare and important manuscript.... It took a while to decipher the handwriting, since it is an ancient script.

What did Rabbi Aryeh Kaplan discover when he translated the text? He found a method for converting Creation Time to Human Time. He also found that Rabbi Isaac ben Samuel, in his work *Otzar HaChaim*, was the first to imply that the universe is billions of years old—at a time when prevalent thought was that the universe was thousands of years in age. Rabbi Isaac ben Samuel arrived at this conclusion by distinguishing between "solar years" and "divine years," herein described as Human Time and Divine Time.

Moving through the steps illustrated in Figure 4.1, we discover the timing of Creation events, applying the work of

Rabbi Isaac ben Samuel, with some refinements. We can then convert the time of these events to Human Time.

The next chapter develops the time conversion process in detail.

[1]   Genesis 1:26.

[2]   Yitzchak Ginsburgh, *The Hebrew Letters- Channels of Creative Consciousness*, (Jerusalem: Gal Einai Publications, 1990), pp. 24–36.

[3]   Yerushalami Peah 6:2.

[4]   Rabbi Moshe Lieber, *Ethics of our Fathers* (New York, Mesorah Publications Ltd, 2003), Chapter 1:1.

[5]   Babylonian Talmud, Sanhedrin 38b.

[6]   Joseph Jacobs, S. Horovitz, Midrah, 2002, JewishEncyclopedia.com.

[7]   Marcus Jastrow, J. Theodor, Bereshit Rabbah, 2002, JewishEncyclopedia.com.

[8]   Midrash Genesis, Rabbah 23

[9]   Michael Friedlander, *Pirkê de Rabbi Eliezer* [part of the oral law]. (Illinois: Varda Books, 2004), Introduction.

[10]   Solomon Schechter and Wilhelm Bacher, Johanan b. Zakkai, 2002, JewishEncyclopedia.com.

[11]   Mishnah (Ab. ii. 8).

[12]   Michael Friedlander, *Pirkê de Rabbi Eliezer* [part of the oral law]. (Illinois: Varda Books, 2004), Chapter 14.

[13]   Joseph Jacobs, Morris Liber, M. Seligsohn, Rashi, 2002, JewishEncyclopedia.com.

[14]   Rabbi Meir Zlotowitz, Bereishis, *Genesis / A New Translation with a Commentary Anthologized from Talmudic Midrashic and Rabbinic Sources* (New York: Mesorah Publications Ltd., 1977), p. 70 on Genesis 1:26.

[15] Nissan Mindel, *Talks and Tales* (New York: Merkos L'inyonei Chinuch, 2003).

[16] Rabbi Meir Zlotowitz, Bereishis, Genesis / A New Translation with a Commentary Anthologized from Talmudic Midrashic and Rabbinic Sources (New York: Mesorah Publications Ltd., 1977), p. 70 on Genesis 1:26.

[17] Zohar I, 117a.

[18] Joseph Jacobs, Isaac Broydé, Zohar, 2002, JewishEncyclopedia.com.

[19] Nissan Mindel, "Rabbi Isaac Luria - The Ari Hakodosh," Chabad-Lubavitch Media Center, 2001–2011, www.chabad.org/library/article_cdo/aid/111878/jewish/Rabbi-Isaac-Luria-The-Ari-Hakodosh.htm

[20] Yitzchak Ginsburgh, "The Development of Kabbalistic Thought," Gal Einai Publication Society, 1996–2011.

[21] Rav Avraham Brandwein, "Gilgul Neshamot - Reincarnation of Souls", 5756, Jerusalem, Translation by Avraham Sutton, www.projectmind.org/exoteric/souls.html

[22] (i) Kaufmann Kohler, M. Seligsohn, Isaac ben Samuel of Acre, 2002, JewishEncyclopedia.com.
(ii) Rabbi Aryeh Kaplan, *The Age of the Universe: A Torah True Perspective* (Rueven Meir Caplan, 2008).

[23] Chaim Joseph David ben Isaac Zerachia Azulai (1724–21 March 1807) was a rabbinical scholar who pioneered the history of Jewish religious writings.

[24] Rabbi Aryeh Kaplan, *The Age of the Universe: A Torah True Perspective* (Rueven Meir Caplan, 2008).

Chapter 5

Conversion of Times

I shall take you out from under the burdens of Egypt ... I shall redeem you with an outstretched arm and with great judgments.[1]

An outstretched arm? Is it possible that God has a tangible arm?

A fundamental belief of those who accept the Bible's teachings is that God does not have a material body.[2] Yet the Bible is full of allusions to God in human terms: his hand, his breath, his arm. Maimonides, an eminent Jewish philosopher and one of the greatest Torah scholars of the Middle Ages, includes God not having a material body as one of the 13 principles of faith[3] (in his Commentary on the Mishnah). He further explains: "The Torah speaks in the language of men." Does the Torah speak in analogies?

It does not.

Every word in the Torah is real and carries deep meaning. God's arm is really an arm. But what does God's arm mean? We simply don't know. Can we gain some insight, hint, or understanding of what God's arm implies by looking at our own arm as the analogy? Yes, by all means.

The Torah is real—our world is the analogy.

To extend the reasoning, what does a Biblical Creation day mean? An earth day is the result of the earth spinning on its axis, making the sun appear to rise, move across the sky, set, and do so again every 24 hours. For astronauts on board the space station, a day (from sunrise to sunrise) is approximately 90 minutes. On the planet Venus, a day is 243 earth days—so very different from a day on earth, and yet still called a day.

Yet, "the Torah speaks in the language of men."

A Creation day is extraordinary, perhaps 2.5 billion years in length. Our earth day is simply an analogy to help us understand what is meant by a creation day.

A computer has an internal clock that runs very fast. In fact, every six months or so we want to buy a new computer, partly because the new one has a faster clock—1 GHz, 2 GHz.... Yet, when we look at the computer screen or when the computer logs the time of our e-mails, it uses time we understand, therefore relying on two different clocks: one clock and time to drive the inner workings of the computer, and another clock and time to communicate with us.

Creation Time is used by God to communicate with us—a concept we can relate to, comprehend, remember, and explain to children. But this is not the time by which the universe operates.

God is above time; past, present, and future are all one to Him.[4] Yet, the action of Creation requires God to contract his infinity and create a clock—a divine clock to keep Divine Time by which the universe operates.

Here on earth, in the midst of physical creation, there is another clock—one for keeping Human Time—as measured by our heartbeat, the sun's shadow, the swing of the pendulum.

Thus, we can now understand the differences among three distinct time measurements:

1. Creation Time is used by God to communicate with us, with its meaning hidden by the human language in which it is expressed, as creation days.

2. Divine Time is the actual time on which the universe operates.

3. Human Time is the time measured by us using our earthly clocks.

Today, the only measurement we rely upon is Human Time. We observe the universe and record those observations using our clocks. Yet before Adam sinned, when God was observing events, He used Divine Time—a special clock invented for this purpose. Nonetheless, He told us the Creation story "in the language of men," using the words "creation days" (i.e., in Creation Time).

This chapter describes all three types of time (Creation, Divine, and Human) and explores the timelines of each to show how we can convert from one type of time to another.

The remainder of this book will then use the conversion factors derived in this chapter to convert the Creation Time of events in Day 6 of the Genesis narrative to Human Time (as measured by scientists), allowing us to compare the creation account of the appearance of humankind to scientific theories and observations of the appearance of humans.

SECTION 1 - CREATION TIME

In this section we first examine Adam as he compares and contrasts with Homo sapiens. We then look at Day 6 to understand the creation timeline and the details of the hour-by-hour events of Day 6 as they pertain to Adam.

Adam and Humankind

Adam, known as the first created man, is pictured by most as a man like others today. However, this is not the case. Adam was nothing like us, physically or spiritually. Only after the sin was he greatly diminished, and so became closer to what we imagine; before the sin he was substantially different.

The Talmud provides descriptions of Adam that include a cosmic being: *"Adam extended from the earth to the firmament ...*

from one end of the earth to the other,"[5] with a mind that could comprehend the universe.[6]

Adam would have been eternal if he had not committed the sin of disobedience. The Midrash teaches that Adam was so different from us today that the very angels thought he was a deity: "*When he was created the angels erred (thinking he was a divine being) and wished to sing 'Holy' before him.*"[7] As we shall see in Chapter 6, Adam was also very different from us spiritually.

The Creation timeline developed below shows that Adam (and Eve) was alive for much of Day 6 hundreds of millions of years ago. However, this does not mean there was a human, in a human form as we know it today, alive at that time. Humanity as we understand it came much later, with the sin. The language employed in this book from this point forward uses the terms "Adam" and "man" interchangeably (representing a special being). The term "human" or "humankind" is used to denote our species, Homo sapiens.

The Creation Timeline

The Creation timeline comprises the six days of Creation, each broken into 24 hours. This six-day period is subsequently followed by 6,000 years of history, followed by the 1,000 years of the seventh millennium,[8] thereby completing the full Biblical timeline. We examine Day 6.

Adam (and humankind that descended from him) is the most important creation—everything is made for him and his kind. Thus, the Talmud provides a detailed account of man and his actions during Day 6, hour by hour.

> *The day consisted of twelve hours. In the first hour, his [Adam's] dust was gathered; in the second, it was kneaded into a shapeless mass. In the third, his limbs were shaped; in the fourth, a soul was infused into him; in the fifth, he arose and stood on his feet;*

in the sixth, he gave [the animals] their names; in the seventh, Eve became his mate; in the eighth, they ascended to bed as two and descended as four [i.e., Cain and Abel were born]; in the ninth, he was commanded not to eat of the tree; in the tenth, he sinned; in the eleventh, he was tried; and in the twelfth he was expelled [from Eden] and departed, for it is written, Man abideth not in honor.[9]

Figure 5.1 illustrates Day 6, which is shown as having one 12-hour period of darkness (shaded) followed by 12 individual daylight hours described above. The numbers signify the hour of the day: 1 is the first hour (typically 6 a.m. to 7 a.m.).

Creation Time	Creation Events
12	
1	Dust was gathered
2	Dust kneaded into shapeless mass; Formation of complex life begins
3	Adam's limbs shaped
4	Soul infused into Adam
5	Adam rose and stood on his feet
6	Adam named the animals
7	Eve was created
8	Cain and Abel born. Garden is planted after man created
9	Adam and Eve are commanded not to eat from the Tree
10	Adam and Eve sinned
11	Adam and Eve were tried
12	Adam and Eve were expelled from the Garden

DAY 6 (hours)

Figure 5.1 Creation Time—Day 6

SECTION 2 - DIVINE TIME

Divine Time is the fundamental inner working clock of the universe.

Divine Time is explained in detail in Annex B where it is shown that one Creation Day is equivalent to 7,000 Divine Years.

SECTION 3 - HUMAN TIME

Human Time is measured with clocks and instruments. In this section we explore its relation to Divine Time and to Creation Time.

What time do humans measure when probing the cosmos with space telescopes, or when dating fossil records?

When God is considered the conscious observer, we must necessarily convert Divine Time to time as experienced by humans (Human Time). The conversion factor is provided for us in Psalms as interpreted in the Talmud: one divine day is 1,000 years of Human Time.[10] Given that a calendar year is 365.25 days (a leap year with one extra day occurs every four years; thus on average, each year is 365 and one-quarter days), then one divine year equates to 365,250 years of Human Time.

In order to derive Human Time from Divine Time we multiply Divine Time by 365,250. Creation Time is converted to Human Time by multiplying it by 7,000 (conversion of Creation Time to Divine Time) and again by 365,250 (conversion of Divine Time to Human Time). One Creation day is therefore equal to 2.56 billion years of Human Time (see Table 5.1). The time conversion formula is very simple:

1 Creation Day = 7000 x 1000 x 365.25 = 2.56 billion years

Once man becomes the conscious observer, the conversion factor becomes one, e.g., one year is one year, and one hour is one hour.

Table 5.1 Human Time vs. Creation Time

Year	365.25 days	
Divine Day	1,000 years in Human Time	
Divine Year	365,250 years in Human Time	= 356.25 x 1,000
Creation Day	7,000 Divine Years	
Creation Day	2.56 billion years in Human Time	= 365,250 x 7,000
Creation hour	106.53 million years in Human Time	= 2.56 BY ÷ 24
Creation second	29,592 years in Human Time	= 106.53 MY ÷ 3600
Creation Day	0.934 x 10^{12} days in Human Time	= 2.56 BY x 365.25

BY = billion years / MY = million years

Exactly when does the simple conversion formula of one Creation day equaling 2.56 billion years apply? When is the beginning of Creation, or by another term the start time? And when is the time when man becomes the conscious observer, that is, the end time.[11]

The Start Time

Clearly God is the conscious observer when creation of the universe starts. However, the physical creation starts on the sunrise of Day 1, or 12 hours into the day.[12] Before this time, nothing physical exists. When we now peer into our telescopes and develop the theory of the Big Bang, we extrapolate back to time zero. This *"in the beginning..."* occurs at precisely 12 hours into Day 1. As such, when we convert Creation Time to Human Time, we start with the first hour of daylight.

The End Time

The conversion from Creation Time to Human Time ends when man becomes the conscious observer.

When does man become the conscious observer? Is it at the end of Day 6, or when man is created, or perhaps some other time?

Prior work[13] has assumed it occurs when Adam is created. When man is first created, he is clearly at one with his Creator. In fact, he is still a composite male and female man, according to the Midrash.[14] Once he is judged and evicted from the Garden of Eden, he is clearly a separate conscious observer of his world.

The transition occurs when Adam sins. It is at this point that Adam separates from his Creator and makes a moral choice of his own. The Biblical text is clear on this point:[15] *"Man has become like the unique One among us, knowing good and bad..."* Rashi elaborates: *"*...unique one among us meaning that he has become unique among the terrestrial ones, just as God is unique among the celestial ones."

In the Talmud we are told that Adam sins during the tenth hour of the day.[16] However, Midrash Rabbah[17] makes it clear that Adam and Eve had to wait a mere three hours to inherit the blessing of Eden for all time; the sin occurred at the very beginning of the tenth hour.

After the tenth hour, time is as we experience it now, and less than 6,000 years have elapsed.

We are now ready to convert from Creation Time to Human Time and reveal what Genesis says about the timelines for the formation of the universe and for the development of life on earth including the appearance of humankind.

The Human Timeline

Figure 5.2 depicts the Human Timeline for Day 6 together with the creation and divine timelines. The third timeline is the Human timeline from zero time at the beginning of the universe until today, 13.7 billion years later. The fourth timeline in the figure is identical to the Human Timeline (the third timeline), with the adaptation that it reports times in reverse, starting at 0 as the current time, and running to the beginning of creation at 13.74 billion years ago. Note that this fourth timeline shows time as zero at Hour 10 of Day 6. The reason is that the time is given in units of billions of years and time, between today and Hour 10, of 5,773 years is therefore inconsequential. Below this Human Timeline the events pertaining to the appearance of life on earth as derived from the study of the fossil record are shown.

Using Figure 5.2, The Genesis One Code[18] demonstrates clear alignment between the times of key events described in the creation narrative as they pertain to the appearance of life on earth, with those derived from scientific observation. Our focus in this book, The Broken Gift, is on the appearance of Homo sapiens. As explained earlier, Adam was a divine being who, as can be seen in Figure 5.2, lived for hundreds of millions of years prior to the sin. During Adam's creation and life, on Day 6, all other complex life appeared on earth. Following the sin, 5,773 years have elapsed as counted according to the Biblical timeline. Adam also lived for the first 930[19] of these years.

We will first explore what exactly happened during Adam's sin and how that may relate to the appearance of Homo sapiens. We then will return to the timeline of Day 6 and examine in detail the timeline of the sin and the appearance of Homo sapiens.

Creation Time (DAY 6 (hours))	Creation Events	Divine Time (thousands of years)	Human Time (from start in billion years)	Human Time (from now running backwards in billion years)	Events from Science
12					
1	Dust was gathered	38500	12.78	0.96	
2	Dust kneaded into shapeless mess; Formation of complex life begins	38792	12.89	0.85	
3	Adam's limbs shaped	39083	13.00	0.75	
4	Soul infused into Adam	39375	13.10	0.64	Cambrian Explosion
5	Adam rose and stood on his feet	39667	13.21	0.53	First fish
6	Adam named the animals	39958	13.32	0.43	Primitive plants. Four-legged animals
7	Eve was created	40250	13.42	0.32	Seeds, plants and trees diversify
8	Cain and Abel born. Garden is planted after man created.	40542	13.53	0.21	Flowering plants Modern birds
9	Adam and Eve are commanded to not eat from the Tree	40833	13.64	0.11	Age of universe 13.7
10	Adam and Eve sinned	41125	13.74	0.0	
11	Adam and Eve were tried	41417			
12	Adam and Eve were expelled from the Garden	41708			
		42000			

Figure 5.2 Timelines - Day 6

[1] Exodus 6:6.

[2] From translation of the full text of the 13 foundations of Jewish belief compiled by Rabbi Moshe ben Maimon; Third Foundation.

[3] Ibid.

[4] Eliezer Zeiger, "Time, Space and Consciousness." BOr HaTorah Vol. 15, ed. Prof. Herman Branover (Israel: SHAMIR, 2005).

[5] Babylonian Talmud, Chagigah 12a.

[6] Howard Schwartz, *Tree of Souls: The Mythology of Judaism* (Oxford University Press, 2004), p. 130.

[7] Midrash, Rabbi Meir Zlotowitz, Bereishis, Genesis / A New Translation with a Commentary Anthologized from Talmudic Midrashic and Rabbinic Sources (New York: Mesorah Publications Ltd., 1977), p. 13.

[8] Zohar VaYera 119a, Ramban on Genesis 2:3 maintain that the seven days of creation correspond to seven millennia of the existence of natural creation. The tradition teaches that the seventh day of the week, Shabbat or the day of rest, corresponds to the Great Shabbat, the seventh millennium (years 6,000–7,000), the age of universal rest.

[9] Babylonian Talmud, Sanhedrin 38b.

[10] *"For a thousand years in your sight are but like yesterday when it is past"* (Psalm 90:4), as interpreted in the Babylonian Talmud, Sanhedrin 97a and 97b.

[11] Historically, authors (see the three following references) have applied a conversion factor from Creation Time to Human Time to the cycles prior to Adam. Here we cannot apply the conversion factor directly to the 7,000-year cycles within each of the six creation days for two reasons: (1) the start time of physical creation is not the beginning of Day 1, and (2) the point in time when God ceases to be the conscious observer does not occur at the end of Day 6. This section

explores the start and end times for the conversion from Creation Time to Human Time.

(i) Avi Rabinowitz and Herman Branover, "The Role of the Observer in Halakhah and Quantum Physics," H. Branover and I. Attia. eds. (Northvale, NJ: *Science in the Light of the Torah: A B'or Ha'Torah Reader*, 1994).

(ii) Rabbi Aryeh Kaplan, *The Age of the Universe: A Torah True Perspective* (Rueven Meir Caplan, 2008).

(iii) Alexander Poltorak, "On the Age of the Universe," BOr HaTorah Vol. 13, ed. Prof. Herman Branover (Israel: SHAMIR, 1999).

[12] The day in the Genesis text is described as a 24-hour period from evening to sunset. We learn from the details about Day 6 (described in the Talmud) that God works at making physical items for a period of 12 hours. Further, since the work for Day 6 is finished at sunset, he must work the second 12 hours of the day, i.e., the daylight hours.

By extension we deduce that the main work in Days 1 through 5 is also done during the second 12 hours of the day. This assumption is reinforced by the general concept that God follows his own Torah, where the labor laws also specify that the norm is to work during the 12 daylight hours (although work at night is allowed). The Talmud provides the employment rules for workers where no other arrangement has been made; workers are to leave the house at sunrise, go to work, work until sunset, and return in their own time after sunset (Babylonian Talmud, Baba-Mezi'a, Chapters 6 and 7).

[13] (i) Avi Rabinowitz and Herman Branover, "The Role of the Observer in Halakhah and Quantum Physics," H. Branover and I. Attia. eds. (Northvale, NJ: *Science in the Light of the Torah: A B'or Ha'Torah Reader*, 1994).

(ii) Rabbi Aryeh Kaplan, *The Age of the Universe: A Torah True Perspective* (Rueven Meir Caplan, 2008).

(iii) Alexander Poltorak, "On the Age of the Universe," BOr HaTorah Vol. 13, ed. Prof. Herman Branover (Israel: SHAMIR, 1999).

(iv) Alexander Poltorak, "The Age of the Universe Using the Many-Worlds Interpretation," BOr HaTorah Vol. 18, ed. Prof. Herman Branover (Israel: SHAMIR, 2008).

[14] Midrash, Rabbi Meir Zlotowitz, Bereishis, *Genesis / A New Translation with a Commentary Anthologized from Talmudic Midrashic and Rabbinic Sources* (New York: Mesorah Publications Ltd., 1977), p. 72 on Genesis 1:27.

[15] Genesis 3:22 and commentary.

[16] Babylonian Talmud, Sanhedrin 38b.

[17] Exodus Midrash Rabbah 32:1.

[18] Daniel Friedmann, *The Genesis One Code* (Inspired Books, 2012), Chapter 8.

[19] Genesis 5:5.

Chapter 6

Adam

When he [Adam] was created the angels erred [thinking he was a divine being] and wished to sing 'Holy' before him.[1]

Adam doesn't sound much like you and me, does he?

Where did he live? Who, or perhaps what, was he? What happened to him when he sinned? What was the impact of his sin on the world?

These are the questions we'll explore in this chapter in order to understand our origins from the Biblical and mystical perspective.

Adam in the Garden of Eden

As we saw in Figure 5.2, Adam was completed at the end of hour 5, 427 million years ago (Ma). We learn from the text of Genesis that prior to man's completion, there was no vegetation, *"and all the herb of the field had not yet sprouted, for God had not sent rain upon the earth and there was no man to work the soil."*[2] Then we are told that, when man was completed, he was placed in the Garden of Eden, where he remained until his expulsion after the sin, 5,773 years ago (as of 2013).

> *God planted a garden toward the east, in Eden; and there He placed the man whom He had formed. And God caused to sprout from the ground every tree that was pleasing to the sight and good for food; the Tree of Life also in the midst of the garden, and the Tree of the Knowledge of Good and Bad.*[3]

Where was this Garden?

The Garden of Eden

Some clues as to the location of the garden are obtained from the Midrashim, which state the following:

1. God created Adam where Jerusalem's temple would later stand, and took him from there and placed him in the garden.[4]

2. Adam drank from the waters at the source of the Euphrates, which flowed from under the Tree of Life in the center of the garden.[5]

3. God gave Adam the cave of Makpelah (located in Hebron just south of Jerusalem), which was near the gate of the garden, as his burial place.[6]

4. On the day he sinned, Adam immersed himself in the Gichon River (thought to be in Ethiopia), and remained there for a full seven weeks.[7]

Thus we see that the Garden did not include Jerusalem, nor Hebron, and in fact, was east of these two cities. Furthermore, the center of the Garden was near the center of the Arabian Peninsula where the Euphrates flows. In addition, it was close to, or encompassed, some of Ethiopia. More clues as to the general area of the garden can be obtained directly from the Genesis text: *"God planted a garden in Eden, to the East..."*[8] *A river issues forth from Eden to water the garden, and from there it is divided and becomes four headwaters."*[9]

The commentaries interpret that the river overflows and waters the garden without need for man or his toil, and the excess water flowing out of the garden forms four parts, each becoming a river's head.[10]

The four rivers are thought to be as follows:[11]

1. Pishon—either the Nile (Egypt) or the Ganges (India)

2. Gichon—identified with Ethiopia

3. Chidekel—the Tigris

4. Euphrates.

If we are going to decipher the clues provided by these rivers, we must first understand how is it possible that these geographies—Ethiopia, the Arabian Peninsula, and India or Egypt—all share headwaters.

Today we know that the rigid outermost shell of our planet is composed of different sections that move relative to one another. Plate tectonics is a scientific theory that describes this large-scale motion of Earth's lithosphere (the outer part of the earth, consisting of the crust and upper mantle, approximately 100 km thick). The theory builds on the older concepts of continental drift, developed during the first decades of the 20th century. It was accepted by the majority of the geo-scientific community in the early 1960s. The lithosphere is broken up into what are called tectonic plates. In the case of the Earth, there are currently seven or eight major plates, and many minor plates. These plates move in relation to one another at one of three types of plate boundaries: collision boundary, spreading or diverging boundary, and parallel movement boundary. Earthquakes, volcanic activity, mountain building, and oceanic trench formation occur along these plate boundaries. Scientists have worked out the position of the plates throughout time. It turns out that when the Garden was planted and Adam placed in it, about 420Ma, the plates were such that Ethiopia, the Arabian Peninsula, India, and Egypt were all adjacent to each other and remained so until the present time, except for India—which separated and drifted to its current position starting 160Ma[12] (about an hour and a half prior to the sin). Figure 6.1 shows the world as it was then.[13] Note that the topography has changed dramatically since the continents were arranged, as per Figure 6.1; most of today's mountain ranges developed after this time.[14]

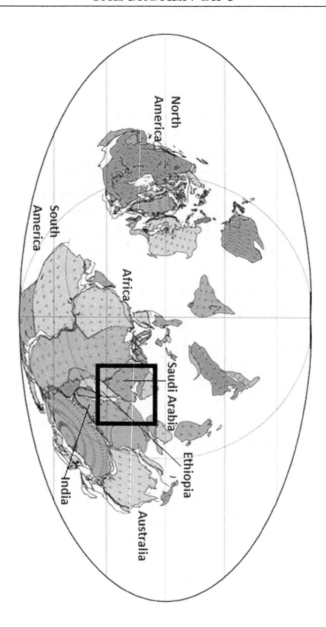

Figure 6.1 The Position of Continents and Garden 420Ma

Now we can put all the evidence together and see that the Garden was just east of Jerusalem, extended perhaps as far south as Ethiopia, and centered in the Arabian Peninsula. The black box outline in Figure 6.1 illustrates the likely position of the Garden. The Garden's southern border corresponds to where modern humans left Africa. The plates have moved such that the Garden remained reasonably close to the equator for its entire history of 420 million years.

Now that we have established where Adam lived and how this location compares to the first modern humans, let's try to understand what he was like before and after the sin.

Adam

To understand who Adam was, we must examine how he came to be. The Genesis account contains acts of creation ("God Created") and acts of formation ("God said, 'Let us make,'" or "form," or "separate," or "bring forth" etc.). Creation is the divine act of making something from nothing (such as a magician seemingly pulling a handkerchief out of thin air). Formation refers to taking something that already exists and changing it into something else (e.g., building a table from wood). There are only three acts of creation mentioned in the Genesis narrative, with most acts being formations.

We have seen in the Creation timeline (Figure 5.2) that Adam's body was *made* over a period of three hours. In the fourth hour his soul was breathed into him. The making of Adam's body is described in similar[15] terms as the making of animals:

"God had formed out of the ground every beast of the field..."[16]
"God formed the man from the dust from the ground..."[17]

The Midrash goes as far as telling us that *"He [God] provided him [Adam] with a tail, like an animal, but subsequently removed it from him for the sake of his dignity."*[18]

However, Adam was a creation, a uniquely human and special creation consisting of a body formed from *"the dust from the ground"* and a soul: *"and He blew into his nostrils the soul of life; and man became a living being."*[19] The way Adam's soul comes into being is contrasted to the way the rest of the created world comes in to being: the soul is blown into Adam; the rest of creation is spoken into being (*"and God said"*). What is the difference between blowing and speaking? Blowing is unconstrained; whereas, speaking is the result of constraining the breath to create a sound. The soul is blown into Adam: thus, it contains pure, essential, and unclothed Divinity.

The Midrash provides details of Adam's uniquely human attributes:

> *He* [God] *created him* [Adam] *with four attributes of the higher beings* [angels] *and four attributes of the lower beings* [animals]. [The four attributes of] *the higher beings are: he stands upright, like the ministering angels; he speaks, like the ministering angels; he understands, like the ministering angels; and he sees* [i.e., he can direct his gaze at an object sideways without turning his head], *like the ministering angels. Yet does not a dumb animal see! But his one* [man] *can see from the side. He* [Adam] *has four attributes of the lower beings: he eats and drinks, like an animal; procreates, like an animal; excretes, like an animal; and dies, like an animal.... Therefore, I will create him of the upper and of the lower elements: if he sins he will die; while if he does not sin, he will live.*[20]

Thus, Adam was like an animal in its bodily requirements with the exception that he could have lived forever if he had not sinned. The uniquely human characteristics that come about from Adam's creation are both physical and mental or spiritual. Physically, man is the only bipedal being, that is stands upright. Although there were early bipedal precursors of Homo sapiens, there are no living animals that stand upright all the time. Many animals have good peripheral vision; some better than man, but man has the best peripheral vision in stereo.

The spiritual differences are understanding and language. Understanding is best described as the ability to learn from the past and from others, and to plan into the future. Language is a uniquely human attribute. In Genesis 2:19, where it is described that Adam named the animals, the "Torah reveals that language is actually a miraculous gift from God to the first man and his descendants."[21] The creation of the universe came about through speech: *"By the word of God, the Heavens were made."*[22] And the creation of man, himself a microcosm of the world, was similarly via becoming a creature of speech. The Torah relates how God breathed into Adam a soul of life transforming him into *"a living being,"*[23] which is interpreted as meaning "a speaking spirit."[24] Speech, the point of connection between body and soul, is what defines humanity.[25]

The Torah teaches that by observing nature we can begin to understand the creation. After a lifetime of observing primates, Jane Goodall came to the same conclusion as to the spiritual difference between humans and other primates.

> Our study of the chimpanzees has helped to pinpoint not only the similarities between them and us, but also those ways in which we are most different. Admittedly we are not the only beings with personalities, reasoning powers, altruism and emotions like joy and sorrow; nor are we the only beings capable of mental as well as physical suffering. But our intellect has grown mightily in complexity since the first time men branched off from the ape-man stock since 2 million years ago. And we, and **only we, have developed a sophisticated spoken language.** For the first time in evolution, a species evolved that was able to teach it's young **about**

objects and events not present, to pass on wisdom gleaned from the successes—and the mistakes—of the past, to make plans for the distant future, to discuss ideas so that they could grow, sometimes out of all recognition, through the combined wisdom of the group. [26] [Author emphasis added.]

The Sin

Adam was around for 427 million years before the sin, and for another 930 years after the sin. What exactly was this sin, and what happened to Adam as a result of it?

During the last hour prior to the sin, or the last 100 million years, a series of events occurred whereby Eve and then Adam disobeyed the commandment to not eat from the Tree of the Knowledge of Good and Bad.

Prior to Adam's eating from the tree, good and evil were distinct entities. It was clear what was good and what was evil, just as today it is clear what is water and what is fire. After Adam ate from the tree the distinction between good and evil got blurred. How so?

Torah conceives of good and evil as opposite poles on the continuum of morality. This means that any situation or entity in life contains elements of both good and evil. This blurring leads to moral struggle. [27]

> Eating the forbidden fruit caused man's psyche to become overtly self-conscious and egocentric. His sensation of good is no longer pure and divine but a mixture of good and evil; he considers something good only if it is self-gratifying. If this attitude is left unchecked, the evil will eventually swallow up the good; one's appreciation for good—and even belief that anything can truly *be* good—will evaporate. This in

turn will engender a feeling of bitterness toward life as one comes to blame others for life's disappointments and suffering. Having thus placed the cause of his suffering outside his sphere of influence, a person views himself as a helpless victim of circumstance and malevolence.[28]

But what exactly happened, and how exactly did Adam change as he committed the sin? Genesis 3 relates the events that occurred over the span of an hour. A complex dialogue ensued between Eve and the serpent, which led Eve to eat from the tree. This dialogue took most of the hour, and you might wonder where Adam was while all this was ensuing? The Midrash explains:

> *Now where was Adam during this conversation? ... He had engaged in intercourse and then fallen asleep. God took him and led him all around the world showing him which land was fit for agriculture and planting trees.*[29]

Adam returns to the scene, Eve partakes of the fruit and becomes hysterical, as she realizes she is now mortal. Eating from the fruit reaped the natural consequence of bringing death into the world, as it says in Genesis: *"the day you eat of it, you shall surely die."*[30] In fact, Eve's name in Hebrew was originally intended to be Chayah, which means "the living soul" and connotes eternal life. After she sinned, Adam called Eve "Chavah," which means "the mother of mortal life."[31] The Midrash explains how Eve, after realizing her mortality and thinking God might provide Adam a new wife, convinced Adam to eat: *"It took tears and lamentations on her part to prevail upon Adam to take the step. Not yet being satisfied, she gave from the fruit to all living beings that they, too, might be subject to death."*[32]

Thus, right at the end of the hour Adam partook from the fruit. We will examine the exact timeline of his sin in a later chapter; here we will remain focused on what happened.

The Physical Impact of the Sin on Adam and Eve

As we saw in Chapter 5 section 1, Adam was a divine being. We can't actually envision exactly what he was like physically, but we do know he was greatly changed by the sin. The Midrash gives us some detail as to what was "taken away" from Adam:

> ...*his lustre, his immortality, his height, the fruit of the earth, the fruit of the trees...Height, for he originally filled the whole world, and now he was small enough to hide among the trees (height reduced to 100 cubits). The fruit of earth and trees reduced for these originally produced in one day.*[33]

In fact, Genesis elaborates on the sin's impact on the earth and therefore, on what Adam would have to do for a living (after enjoying no need for physical exertion in Eden)

> *To Adam He said ... accursed is the ground because of you; through suffering shall you eat of it all the days of your life. Thorns and thistles shall it sprout for you, and you shall eat the herb of the field. By the sweat of your brow shall you eat bread....*[34]

The commentaries interpret the meaning of these words for us: for Adam's sake the earth will yield harvest, but only in scant measure;[35] no longer will the land just produce—now it will require work to yield produce;[36] when you plant, the earth shall bring forth plants that require preparation in order to be edible (prior, the food was readably edible);[37] and you will be forced to eat herbs rather than the fruits of the garden.[38]

Eve, being the other half of original single male and female creation, also changed dramatically. She was assigned the following curses: *"the afflictions arising from menstruation and the tokens of virginity; the affliction of conception in the womb; and the affliction of childbirth; and death."*[39]

All these curses show that Adam and Eve changed to have similar physical characteristics and experiences as we have today, certainly relating to eating, childbearing, and death. However, some major differences remained. Adam was still more than 40 meters in height (100 cubits), and both Adam and Eve lived to 930 years; their direct blood descendants (as mentioned in Genesis) also lived very long lives.

We will have to wait until the next chapter to understand the physical relationship between Adam and us, Homo sapiens. First we must explore what happened to Adam and Eve spiritually.

The Spiritual Impact of the Sin on Adam and Eve

Man's soul[40] is a bridge between his experiences in the physical world and his experience of God. The soul has two components: the animalistic soul and the intellectual soul. The animalistic soul is mainly emotional and contains some intellect to help understand what is good for it and to attain what it wants, e.g., health. The intellectual soul is rational and cerebral. The animalistic soul craves and focuses on bodily needs and pleasures. Nonetheless, the supernal intent is that the animalistic soul be refined, and its power to crave be used for good. This refinement is achieved by the intellectual soul "arguing", using the power of the intellect, with the animalistic soul to do what is right. Thus, the two components of the soul are usually in conflict, and it is this conflict that gives us our free will to choose between right and wrong, usually represented by the intellectual and animalistic souls respectively. It is only humanity that possesses an intellectual soul. Animals have just an animalistic soul.

Adam's soul was very special. When God breathed into him a living soul, the roots of all souls that would descend from Adam (i.e., of all humanity) were implanted within him. Rabbi Issac Luria provides exquisite detail on Adam's soul. Anatomically, Adam's soul consisted of 613 (the number of commandments in the Five Books of Moses) major soul roots. Each of these in turn consisted of 613 small roots, and each of these, of 600,000 individual souls or sparks (of God). Multiplying these three numbers, we get approximately 225 billion individual souls.[41] We will return to this fascinating number in the concluding chapter.

What happened to Adam's soul when he lost his free will battle, disobeyed God, and sinned?

Rabbi Issac Luria[42] provides a dramatic explanation of Adam's fall. According to him, if Adam had fulfilled his mission through contemplative action and deep meditation until the end of the sixth day, the living chain between God and creation would have been completed, and the power of evil totally overcome. But his fall caused the unity of his soul to be shattered. The fate of the fragments had any of three possible outcomes, depending on their purity.

Those soul-elements of high rank, called the "upper light," which refused to participate in his sin, departed for above, and will not return to the world until the time of redemption in the Messianic Era.

Other soul-elements remained in Adam even after his stature was reduced from cosmic to mundane dimensions; these were holy souls that did not fall off him.

The vast majority of soul-elements that were in Adam "fell" into the depths of the klipot (lit. peel for *shell*—word used to describe coverings of impurity).

The 6,000-years of history post-Adam's sin are cosmically there for these later two groups of souls to be rectified, or in

Hebrew, achieve their tikkun (Hebrew for rectification). How so? These souls are to be incarnated into human beings who, by positive deeds during their lives, will rectify a particular soul spark.

Those souls in the second group (that remained in Adam) were relatively large and special souls. They entered bodies of future beings through direct hereditary transmission. But what role did the souls of Eve, Cain, and Abel, who were all alive prior to the sin, play? The sources explain[43] that when Adam and his wife Eve sinned, as well as Cain and Abel, their children, all the soul sparks, became mixed together. Accordingly, sparks of Adam combined with those of Cain and Abel, and sparks of Abel with Adam's and Cain's, etc. These major souls were then passed on to Adam's other children, to his children's children, and so on to Noah and his three children, ten generations later. What does major soul mean? Exploring this answer will lead us to understand what was different about Adam's direct descendants, the people described in Genesis.

Those souls that fell and were covered by the klipot were relatively minor souls and were now available, for the first time in history, to be incarnated into beings—but not Adam's direct descendants. What beings, then? Exploring this answer will lead us to understand our main issue—the relation between Adam and us, Homo sapiens.

In the next chapter we will attempt to answer these last two questions, and we will come to grips with the relation between Adam and all who came after him. Then we will return to the timeline on which all the events described herein occurred.

---

[1]   Midrash, Rabbi Meir Zlotowitz, Bereishis, *Genesis / A New Translation with a Commentary Anthologized from Talmudic Midrashic and Rabbinic Sources* (New York, Mesorah Publications Ltd., 1977), p. 13.

[2] Genesis 2:5.

[3] Genesis 2:8 and 2:9.

[4] Rabbi Yaakov Culi, *The Torah Antology*, (NY: Moznaim Publishing Corporation, 1988), p. 248.

[5] Rabbi Yaakov Culi, *The Torah Antology*, (NY: Moznaim Publishing Corporation, 1988), pp. 282–283.

[6] Rabbi Yaakov Culi, *The Torah Antology*, (NY: Moznaim Publishing Corporation, 1988), p. 284.

[7] Ibid.

[8] Genesis 2:8.

[9] Genesis 2:10.

[10] Rabbi Meir Zlotowitz, Bereishis, *Genesis / a new translation with a commentary anthologized from Talmudic Midrashic and Rabbinic sources* (NY: Mesorah Publications Ltd., 1977), p. 96.

[11] Rabbi Meir Zlotowitz, Bereishis, *Genesis / a new translation with a commentary anthologized from Talmudic Midrashic and Rabbinic sources* (NY: Mesorah Publications Ltd., 1977), pp. 97–98.

[12] L.A. Lawver, I.W.D. Dalziel, and L.M. Gahagan, "2006 Atlas of Plate Reconstructions (750 Ma to Present Day)", Univ. of Texas Institute for Geophysics, March 8, 2007.

[13] Ibid.

[14] Earth's history is marked by three great periods when mountains were formed. The first occurred more than 400 million years ago. Some mountain ranges in the eastern part of North America are remnants of that period. The second period was around 300 million years ago, when some of the massifs of Europe and central Asia were formed. The last period occurred barely 50 million years ago, when the Alps and the Himalayas were formed. http://www.ikonet.com/en/visualdictionary/static/us/mountains.

[15] Although the body of animals and Man are "formed" from the "ground", there is still a difference. Man is formed

form the "dust from the ground", meaning from fine particles versus just from the ground, meaning a clump of dirt. Thus, the use of the word dust indicates that unlike animals man: (1) is a compilation of varied and even opposing traits versus being fairly homogenous, (2) is made from the top part of the ground giving him an ability to use his traits toward spiritual aims, etc. see Mendel Weinbach, Reuven Subar, *The Essential Malbim* (New York: Mesorah Publications Ltd., 2009), pp. 25–29.

[16] Genesis 2:19.

[17] Genesis 2:7.

[18] H. Freedman and M. Simon, Eds., *Midrash Rabbah Genesis*, (New York: Soccino Press, 1985), XIV. 10, p. 118.

[19] Genesis 2:7.

[20] H. Freedman and M. Simon, Eds., *Midrash Rabbah Genesis*, (New York: Soccino Press, 1985), VIII. 11, p. 61.

[21] Mendel Weinbach, Reuven Subar, *The Essential Malbim* (New York: Mesorah Publications Ltd., 2009), pp. 46–47.

[22] Psalms 33:6.

[23] Genesis 2:7.

[24] Rabbi Meir Zlotowitz, Bereishis, *Genesis / a new translation with a commentary anthologized from Talmudic Midrashic and Rabbinic sources* (NY: Mesorah Publications Ltd., 1977), Onkeles on Genesis 2:7, p. 92.

[25] Rabbi Osher Chaim Levene, "Parshas Chayei Sarah - Shevuah: I Solemnly Swear", Torah.org 2005. torah.org/learning /livinglaw/5766/chayeisarah.htm

[26] Jane Goodall with Phillip Berman, *Reason for Hope - a Spiritual Journey*, (New York: Warner Books Inc., 2000) pp. 93–94.

[27] Rabbi Yitzchak Ginsburgh, "Kabbalah and Psychology, Anxiety Relief, The Kabbalah Approach to Mental Health, Part 36, Good and Evil" Gal Einai Institute (2004).

[28] Yitzchak Ginsburgh, *The Mystery of Marriage* (Israel: Gal Einai Publication Society, 1999), pp. 11–12.

[29] H. Freedman and M. Simon, Eds., Midrash Rabbah Genesis, (New York: Soccino Press, 1985), XIX. 3, p. 149.

[30] Genesis 2:17; Malbim's explanation.

[31] Yitzchak Ginsburgh, "Parshat Chukat: Why Is There Death in the World?", Gal Einai Publication Society, 1996.

[32] Rabbi Meir Zlotowitz, Bereishis, *Genesis / A New Translation with a Commentary Anthologized from Talmudic Midrashic and Rabbinic Sources* (New York, Mesorah Publications Ltd., 1977), Midrash Genesis 3:7, p. 120.

[33] H. Freedman and M. Simon, Eds., *Midrash Rabbah Genesis,* (New York: Soccino Press, 1985), XII. 6, p. 91.

[34] Genesis 3:17.

[35] Rabbi Meir Zlotowitz, Bereishis, *Genesis / A New Translation with a Commentary Anthologized from Talmudic Midrashic and Rabbinic Sources* (New York: Mesorah Publications Ltd., 1977), Ibn Ezra; Radak, p. 132.

[36] Ibid. Midrash Aggadah; Radak, p. 133.

[37] Ibid. Rashi, p. 133.

[38] Ibid. Radak, p. 134.

[39] Michael Friedlander, *Pirkê de Rabbi Eliezer* (Illinois: Varda Books, 2004), Chapter 14.

[40] Rabbi Yitzchak Ginsburgh, *Anatomy of the Soul* (New York: Dwelling Place Publishing, December 2008).

[41] Gershom Scholem, *Kabbalah* (New York: Times books, 1978), p. 162. 613 x 613 x 600,000 = 225 billion

[42] Gershom Scholem, *Kabbalah* (New York, Times books, 1978), pp. 152–168.

[43] From the teachings of Rabbi Yitzchak Luria, "Intermingled Souls," Gate of Reincarnations: Chapter Thirty,

Section 3; Translation and Commentary by Perets Auerbach, www.chabad.org/kabbalah/article_cdo/aid/1536737/jewish/Intermingled-Souls-303.htm

Chapter 7

The Need for Humanity

Homo sapiens - the only surviving hominin; species to which modern man belongs; bipedal primate having language and ability to make and use complex tools; brain volume of at least 1,400 cc.

The bad news is that Adam sinned. The good news is that because of his sin we are needed, and therefore, we exist.

Adam had the soul of all humanity implanted in him. When he sinned, his soul shattered into billions of sparks, or individual souls, which as a result of the sin needed to be rectified. Some were to be rectified by being passed on hereditarily to Adam's children. The majority had to be rectified by being incarnated into beings. Since the souls to be incarnated originated from a primordial divine being whose soul had shattered, the derived souls, or sparks, retained their connection with the root soul. Hence, we have souls bound together by a common purpose, because they came from the same original soul. The purpose of these individual souls is therefore defined by that particular aspect, a particular role to be played in the Divine plan of cosmic progress and unfolding. Thus, people with individual destinies are striving to achieve their spiritual mission as represented in the original divine destiny from which their soul derives.

Homo Sapiens

But into what are these souls supposed to be incarnated?

Have you ever wondered where all the people in Genesis came from? The simple answer is from Adam. But this does not make sense. There are too many people appearing too soon in the story for all to come from Adam. For example, Cain kills Able before Genesis states that anyone else is born. When Cain is punished and banished by God, he has to be protected from other people: *"I [Cain] must be a wanderer on earth; whomever meets me will kill me! ... God placed a mark upon Cain, so that none that met him might kill him."*[1] What other people? No one has come along yet. Cain then goes on to marry, have a son, and become *"a city builder and he called the name of the city after the name of his [first]son Enoch."*[2] He became a city builder—for whom? Adam's next son Seth is not born until many years later. Further on in Genesis, we hear of other people and giants. Where do these beings come from? And why are the characters named in Genesis (up to Noah) able to live for hundreds of years, many to almost one thousand years of age? There are no fossils of past beings that provide evidence of them having lived more than 100 years, nor any humans today living much past 100. What's going on?

Had Adam not sinned, there would have been no need for other people to exist to rectify the soul sparks that resulted from his sin. The logical explanation to the above questions is that as a result of Adam embarking in the sin, Homo sapiens became a necessity in the Divine plan. They first came into existence as anatomically modern humans but with no human soul. When Adam's soul shattered and the soul sparks became available, they began to be incarnated into these anatomically modern humans, who as a result from this point on contained a human soul, and thus become behaviorally modern humans, exhibiting modern behaviors such as language.

Adam caused the need for Homo sapiens, and Adam supplied the soul sparks for them to become behaviorally modern. It is interesting to note that after a lifetime of observing primates, Jane Goodall came close to conceiving the ideas described herein by understanding that there were animals that looked like humans which at some point became behaviorally modern humans:

> I imagined God, looking down on creation, evaluating human progress and deciding the time had come when these sons and daughters of His were ready to be made aware, truly aware, of who they were.[3]

We will explore the exact timeline for events leading to modern humans in the next chapter. However, for now it should be understood that time does not change from Creation Time (with God as the conscious observer) to Human Time until after the sin is complete. Adam, on the other hand, experiences the changes and the shattering of his soul as he performs the sin, by exercising his free will. Thus, Homo sapiens came into existence and became behaviorally modern while time was still in Creation Time, well before 5,773 years ago (as of 2013). On the other hand, the events relating to Cain all begin 5,773 years ago. Thus, by the time Cain murdered his brother Homo sapiens were roaming the world—numbering in the millions.[4] These millions of Homo sapiens explain all the people in Genesis other than Adam's direct descendants.

The above explanations are an attempt to reconcile the existence of Homo sapiens for hundreds of thousands of years, and their acquisition of modern human behavior, with the Bible and Adam. Although this is a new reconciliation, it borrows heavily from traditional sources. Below is a paraphrase from the Shaar HaGilgulim by the Arizal, provided so that the reader can compare and contrast what has been explained above with the work of a great sage.

The Arizal explains that Adam had a universal soul that included all the souls of mankind in a higher unity. This is why even one action on his part could have such a powerful effect.

After he ate from the Tree of Knowledge of Good and Evil, his soul fragmented into thousands and thousands of sparks that subsequently became incarnated in every single human being who was ever born, is alive now and will live in the future. The main role of these individuals is to elevate the soul sparks to bring about the tikkun (rectification) that Adam was to do alone.[5]

A rectification that required Adam to nullify his ego and obey the command not to eat for 3 more hours until the end of day 6.

Adam's Direct Descendants and Their Life Spans

Unlike coexistent Homo sapiens, Adam's direct descendants had major, inclusive souls.[6] All souls require rectification; the larger the soul the larger the rectification required and the longer the process takes. Thus, Adam's direct descendants needed more time and thus a longer lifespan to mend their major souls.

What happened post-Noah to shorten the lifetimes of Adam's hereditary descendants?

> Originally, God assigned great tasks to the antediluvian [prior to the Flood] generations and at the same time equipped them with commensurately greater souls.... He granted each human a certain number of days...approximately 300,000 [820 years].... After the failure which resulted in the deluge, all of this was restricted in order to help us achieve what is expected of us in a lifespan averaging 70 years.[7]

Their souls were diminished and fragmented into minor souls in order to make the work of tikkun easier for each person. Thus, these smaller souls required less work, and as a consequence, those incarnated with them had shorter lives.

From a few generations post-Flood there is thus no difference in souls; all are about the same size requiring about the same lifespan for rectification—the lifetimes we experience. We will return to the Genesis Flood in much more detail in a later chapter.

Homo Sapiens and Apes

Having understood how Homo sapiens came to be and how they differed from Adam and his direct descendants until the Flood, we now explore the relation between Homo sapiens and apes. Although scientists have theorized a common ancestor to early hominins and chimpanzees, and genetic studies[8] have revealed that we share more than 98% of our DNA and almost all of our genes with our closest living relative, the chimpanzee, Biblical sources long before Darwin indicated there was a strong biological relation between humans and other primates.

An Intermediary

The Arizal[9] teaches that between every two levels of reality there is always an intermediate level. An intermediate is meant to unite the two levels, and thus shares characteristics of each. The physical reality consists of mineral (rocks), plant, animal, human, and Divine. Thus there is an intermediary between each of these levels. We have already explored the intermediary between Humans and the Divine: that is, the spiritual element of man.

What about the intermediary between rocks and plants? There is no description in the sources of what this is. However, there are plants that look like rocks. Lithops is a genus of succulent plants. Members of the genus are native to southern Africa. Their name is derived from the ancient Greek words meaning "stone" and "face," referring to the stone-like appearance of the plants. They avoid being eaten by blending in with surrounding rocks and are often known as pebble plants or living stones. Lithops have a pair of leaves that have adapted to efficiently retain whatever moisture becomes available to them. To minimize evaporation, the leaves are so truncated that they have lost the appearance of a normal leaf and are rounded like a pebble.

The intermediate between the plant and animal kingdoms is a creature called the *Adney Sadeh* as explained in the Mishnah.[10] The Mishnah is a legalistic text and does not deal with mythical creatures. Therefore, it must be assumed that the *Adney Sadeh* did exist at one time, and the rabbis of the Talmud were familiar with it, even though it has since become extinct. Is there a source for this creature in other literature? In his book[11] *The Vegetable Lamb of Tartary* (1887), Henry Lee describes a similar creature believed to be both a true animal and a living plant. He investigates texts written around 0 CE tracing myths about the creature and concludes it did exist.

What is the intermediary between animals and humans? You guessed it — the monkey. The Arizal explicitly states this in his works hundreds of years before the idea appears in the secular literature (see Chapter 2: Human Evolution).[12]

As every intermediate has two sides, one aspect of the monkey relates to its animalistic tendencies, and the other aspect relates to its human similarities. The actual Hebrew word used in the literature as the intermediary is *kof*. Although kof is translated as monkey, the term either "ape" or "primate" (excluding humans) may be more appropriate.[13]

The biological order of primates includes about 180 mammalian species. Primates are characterized as having thumbs that can touch each of the other fingers and thereby function in grasping objects. In addition, primates have shortened snouts, with eyes on the front rather than on the side of the head, thereby allowing for stereoscopic (three-dimensional) vision. Primate gestation is lengthy, with one birth at a time, and with an extended juvenile period of dependency during which there is an emphasis on learned behavior and complex social interactions. As we move along the chain of primates closer to humans, we encounter apes. Apes have no tails and generally have a larger body weight than most other primates. They have a more upright body posture and a broad chest, rely more on vision than on smell, and have a broad nose rather than a snout. Apes have a larger brain relative to their body size than do other primates. Gorillas, orangutans, and chimpanzees are categorized as apes. The theory of evolution postulates that through repeated speciation, early primates split into New World monkeys (about 35 million years ago), Old World monkeys (about 25 million years ago), and then into hominoids. The hominoids differed from the Old World monkeys in having longer arms and no tail. Over the next 20 million years or so, the gibbons and three groups of what are termed the great apes— orangutans, gorillas, and chimpanzees— separated from the line that eventually led to us.

The Torah states that we are a divine creation. But indeed, studying humans and other primates would lead us to the conclusion that we are very similar, anatomically and biologically, since other primates are intermediaries between us and the rest of the animals.

Having understood the need for humanity, along with its origins and relationship to other primates, we now look at the timeline over which Adam's sin occurred. With this timeline we will be able to compare and contrast the Biblical with the scientific account of humanity.

---

[1]   Genesis 4:14–15.

[2]   Genesis 4:17.

[3]   Jane Goodall with Phillip Berman, *Reason for Hope - a Spiritual Journey*, New York: Warner Books Inc., 2000), p. 51.

[4]   (i) Colin McEvedy and Richard Jones, *Atlas of World Population History*, Puffin Books, London, 1978, pp. 342–351.
(ii)   for summary see U.S. Census Bureau, www.census.gov/population/international/data/idb/worldhis.php.

[5]   Rav Avraham Brandwein, "Gilgul Neshamot, Reincarnation of Souls," 5756, Jerusalem, Translation by Avraham Sutton, www.projectmind.org/exoteric/souls.html.

[6]   Rabbi Chayim Ben Attar (translated by Eliyahu Munk), *Or HaChayim, volume 1 (Genesis)* (New York, Lambada Publishers 1999), Parashat Veyechi.

[7]   Rabbi Chayim Ben Attar (translated by Eliyahu Munk), *Or HaChayim, volume 1 (Genesis)* (New York, Lambada Publishers 1999), p. 390.

[8]   The Chimpanzee Sequencing and Analysis Consortium, "Initial sequence of the chimpanzee genome and comparison with the human genome," *Nature*, 437, pp. 69–87 (1 September 2005).

[9]   Yitzchak Ginsburgh, "De-evolution of the Human - A Mystical View on Primates," Gal Einai Publication Society, 1996.

[10]   Mishnah Kela'im (8:5).

[11]   Henry Lee, *The Vegetable Lamb of Tartary* (London: Sampson Low, Marston, Searle, & Rivington, 1887), p. 2.

[12]   Yitzchak Ginsburgh, "De-evolution of the Human - A Mystical View on Primates," Gal Einai Publication Society, 1996.

[13]   H. Babich, "The Kof, Reverse Evolution, and the Adnei Ha-Sadeh," Torah Science Foundation, 2001, www.torahscience.org/natsci/animal.htm.

Chapter 8

The Timeline for the Appearance of Homo Sapiens

What was Adam thinking? God had commanded him personally to not take a specific action, and here he was disobeying. How long did it take him to make the decision to eat the fruit? What process did he go through to make such a rebellious moral decision? Exploring these questions will allow us to construct the exact timeline of the sin.

To grasp these questions, we need to understand three concepts: the making of Adam in the image of God, the creative and moral decision process, and how long this process takes.

In the Image of God

> *And God said, "Let us make man in Our Image, after Our likeness."*[1]

Wait a minute—what is the "image" and "likeness" of God? In Chapter 5 we saw that a fundamental tenet of belief is that God does not have a shape: physical or spiritual. So what is this image/likeness? There are many dimensions to the answer.

Rashi explains *after our likeness* as meaning with the power of understanding and intellect.[2] Ramban interprets the phrase as with moral freedom and free will.[3] Thus, the classic commentaries explain that man alone—in his spiritual resemblance to his Creator—is endowed with reason, a sense of morality, and free will. It is in this vein that man is described as having been created in God's image. The Arizal's interpretation of image/likeness is different, and profoundly deep. He interprets *"Let us make man in Our Image, after Our likeness."* in this manner:

> ...the Godly *Tzelem* [image] refers to the soul of Man. The soul, in other words, is what the Torah calls [the real] Man.[4]

Other writings explain that "in the image of" means that man is made with the same creative process as God.[5]

Thus, if we can understand God's creative process, we will understand man's creative and moral decision-making process.

God's Creative Process

We have already seen a detailed description of how God created his most important work, man:

> *In the first hour, his [Adam's] dust was gathered; in the second, it was kneaded into a shapeless mass. In the third, his limbs were shaped; in the fourth, a soul was infused into him; in the fifth, he arose and stood on his feet.[6]*

God's creative process follows five steps, all equal in duration. In the case of Adam, a most complex creation, each step took one hour. We saw in Chapter 5 and Annex B (*The "Birth" of Adam in Divine Time*) that the actual physical shape of what is being made appears 34.6 minutes into the second hour, or 58% through the second step (see Annex B footnote 18).

The process of creating Adam is an illustration of the general process employed by God. To understand this process we first explore God's essential name.

God's Names

God is referred to throughout the scriptures by many specific names. What are they? What do they mean? And for that matter, isn't God's essence beyond any name? Yes, it certainly is.

As for His various names, these refer to the different ways in which He reveals Himself in Creation. There are many names for God in the Bible.

In general, there are four categories of names ascribed to God.[7] We need only look at the two highest levels for the purpose of studying the creation narrative, and only the highest level to understand the creative process.

The first category is the essential name *YHWH* (pronounced "Havayah"), also called the Tetragrammaton, meaning the four-letter name. Havayah is the most sacred of God's names and comes closest to expressing His essence in certain contexts. Because of the special sanctity of the four-letter name YHWH, it is not pronounced today and was actually only pronounced within the Holy Temple in Jerusalem.

The second category contains those names that are sacred under Jewish law: Ekyeh (I will be), Kah, Kel, Elokah, Elokim, Tzevakot (Hosts), Shakai (Almighty), Adni (my Master), Akvah, and Ehevi. Each of these names has a specific meaning. The particular name being used reveals to us the role that God is assuming during a particular event in scriptures.

The Creative Steps

To understand the creative process, we need to focus on God's essential name.[8] In Hebrew this name is spelled (as mentioned from right to left) with the letters י, ה, ו, ה. As we saw in Chapter 4, the letters are pictographs. Yud י is shaped in the form of a dot, and is the smallest letter from which all other letters are conceived. It is the quintessential point from which all further existence may develop. It represents the beginning of the creation process, or flash of inspiration.[9] In the human reproductive process this stage corresponds to the sperm. Hei ה symbolizes the process of broadening the initial flash, both in length and depth. It represents the next step in the creative process where the initial concept is worked out and further developed. Within the mind, whatever is being done has taken on some form.[10] In the human reproductive process this stage corresponds to the pregnancy. Vav ו represents the connection between the spiritual and physical, or in the human, the mind and body. Thus the Vav connects the intellectual process of the mind with the body's capabilities to make physical things. With the Vav, finite physical shape is completed for what is being created.[11] In the Human reproductive process this stage and the next correspond to the further development the offspring. With the final Hei, the creation is actualized into its final form.

The letter Hei provides further clues to this creative process.[12] The letter can be seen as graphical representation of the human being's process of making something happen: top horizontal line-thought (steps 1 and 2), vertical line-vocalization (i.e., saying it, step 3) and unattached stub-action (i.e., doing it, step 4). Why is action a stub and not a full line? Because action is not perfectly attached to thought and speech and there can be a gap between thought/speech and deeds. Hei's numerical value is five, and five is also the number of independent vigor. Adam stood up after five hours spent in the Garden of Eden, revealing his physical autonomy. Hei also hints at the five creative steps (including the last one of independent existence).

Table 8.1 illustrates the letters, and their relation to the creative process and to Adam's specific creation.

Table 8.1 Creative Process

Hebrew Letters	Name	Step	Creative step	Analogy to Adam
י	Yud	1	Initial concept	Gathered materials
ה	Hei	2	Broadening the concept	Began to knead and shape
ו	Vav	3	Manifest potential-physical shape	Formed limbs
ה	Hei	4	Actualization	Infused soul of life
		5	Ready to go	Adam stood up

This creative process is also applicable to Adam since he was made in God's image and likeness. Thus, when Adam sins or creates it is the process described above that is in effect.

In summary, the creative process utilized by Adam (and God) is as follows:

1. Five equal steps.

2. The creation attains its initial physical shape (its body in the case of Homo sapiens) 58% through step 2.

3. The creation is actualized (receives its human soul in the case of Homo sapiens) in step 4 and is ready to go or complete by the end of step 4.

4. It becomes an independent entity during step 5 and beyond.

A Moment

How long does this entire process take?

We've seen that the making of man requires five hours. Surely, making an ostensibly simple decision like whether to eat of the forbidden fruit takes less time. From Chapter 6 we know that the whole process of sinning took one hour, and that Adam came into the act right at the end. So how long does it take to make a decision to disobey an order—seconds, right?

Ever wonder why there are so many important 40-day periods in the Bible? Here are some examples:

1. It rained for 40 days and 40 nights when God wanted to cleanse the world and start over. (Genesis 7:12)

2. Noah waited another 40 days after the rain stopped before he opened a window in the Ark. (Genesis 8:6)

3. Embalming required 40 days. (Genesis 50:3)

4. Moses was on the mountain with God for 40 days (twice). (Exodus 24:18, Deuteronomy 10:10)

5. It took the spies 40 days to search out the Promised Land. (Numbers 13:25)

6. Jonah warned the City of Nineveh that they had 40 days until God would overthrow the city. The people repented in those 40 days, and God spared the city. (Jonah 3:4 and 10)

Elsewhere in the Bible we are told that *"God's anger never lasts more than a moment"* (Psalm 30:5): *"His anger lasts but a moment"* (Isaiah 26:20). But wasn't God angry when he brought on the Flood? As we saw in Chapter 5 our experience of anger can be used to understand what the Bible means by God's anger—a temporary separation and withdrawal. What does His anger lasting a moment have to do with 40 days?

It turns out that Moses knew that man[13] could do something in no less than 9.6 seconds or 864/90 seconds. This minimal period of time is the definition of a moment. There are 9,000 such moments in a day. But humans' creative process is derived from God, so a moment for God must also be 9.6 seconds. A divine day is 1,000 Human Time years. What is 9.6 divine seconds, or a moment, for God? A God moment is equivalent to 40 days and 14 hours of Human Time.[14] When the Bible states that God's anger lasts for a moment, it means that it lasts for 40 days of Human Time—like the rain in the Flood narrative. When God has to teach the whole Torah to Moses—how long does it take Him? A moment—40 days in Moses time (Human Time).

What about the little discrepancy of 14 hours? Is it 40 days, or 40 days and 14 hours? Let's look at one of the best documented examples of a God moment—Moses receiving the Torah. Here is the chronology:

1. *God said to Moses, "Ascend to me to the mountain and remain there, that I shall give you the stone tablets…"* (Exodus 24:12)

2. *Moses arrived in the midst of the cloud and ascended the mountain…* (Exodus 24:18)

3. *And I remained on the mountain for forty days and forty nights…* (Deuteronomy 9:9).

4. *It was at the end of forty days and forty nights that God gave me the two stone Tablets, the Tablets of the Covenant…. Then God said to me, "Arise, descend quickly from here…"* (Deuteronomy 9:11–12).

Moses ascends and must arrive prior to sundown; he stays 40 nights and days until sunset on Day 40; he arises the next morning and descends. His total time on the mountain is 40 days and nights, one more night (since he leaves the next morning), and some short extra time of arrival prior to night and departure early in the morning after sunrise. How much extra time? Two hours, according to the calculation of a moment.

Thus, a moment is a very good fit to 40 days and 14 hours. A similar analysis of the Genesis Flood yields the same 40 days and 14 hours for the duration of the rainfall.

For God—a moment, the time it takes for him to teach Torah, or to be angry—is 9.6 seconds; which corresponds to 40 days and 14 hours in Human Time.

Now, how long is a moment for Adam prior to the completion of the sin when he is still keeping Creation Time? A moment for him is 9.6 seconds of Creation Time. What does that correspond to in Human Time? In Chapter 5 we calculated that one day of Creation Time is 2.56 BY of Human Time. The same conversion calculation shows that a moment, or 9.6 seconds of Creation Time, is 284,083 years of Human Time. In other words, it took Adam no less than 284,083 years of human Time to sin.

The Timeline for the Sin

Adam sins in 9.6 seconds. He goes through a process of five equal steps. Approximately 58% of the way into Step 2 the action begins to take form. Since Homo sapiens exist because of the sin, it is at this point that we expect to see the first anatomically modern humans. However, it is not until Step 4 that what is happening is actualized and completed. During this step, therefore, Adam's soul shatters and his soul sparks become available to be incarnated into the Homo sapiens (this parallels Adam receiving his soul during the fourth step of his creation). It is during this fourth step that Homo sapiens receive human souls and thus become behaviorally modern humans who use speech, plan ahead, etc.

Figure 8.1 shows the timeline of the sin.

Corresponding Creation Events	Creation Time — From start of sin (seconds)	Creation Time — Biblical Calendar (years)	Divine Time (years)	Human Time (thousand years)	Human Time (thousand years ago)	Events from Science
			0.00	0	290	
Dust gathered	1.92		0.16	57	233	
Dust kneaded; shape takes form 58% through this Step	3.84		0.31	114	200	Homo sapiens appear by 195 KY ago
Adam's limbs shaped	5.76		0.47	170	176	
Soul infused into Adam	7.68		0.62	227	120	Signs of behavioral modernity
Adam rose and stood on his feet	9.6		0.78	284	63	Modernity established; spread to world
		1000	1		6	
		2000	2		5	
		3000	3		4	
		4000	4		3	
		5000	5		2	
		6000	6		1	
		7000 — M-Era			0	

Figure 8.1 Timelines of the Sin

The first timeline starts 9.6 seconds, or one moment, before the completion of the sin. After this moment, time switches to the Biblical calendar, and 5,773 years have elapsed. We approximate these 5,773 years as 6,000 to keep things simple, keeping in mind that the science dates have uncertainties larger than this approximation. The second timeline shows the equivalent Divine Time, and the third, the equivalent Human Time. Finally, the fourth timeline is just Human Time measured from today backwards, in thousands of years ago. We ascertain from the figure that Homo sapiens experienced the following events:

1. Began to form from whatever preceded them 290,000 years ago

2. Appeared as anatomically modern humans 200,000 years ago (corresponding to 0.58 through step 2)

3. Had become behaviorally modern by 63,000 years ago (although the full process spanned from 120,000 to 63,000 years ago).

Now the soul sparks that had started to incarnate into Homo sapiens during the fourth step, and certainly by the end of the fourth step 63,000 years ago, had a burning desire! Every soul was to fulfill the command given to Adam prior to his sin:

God blessed them and God said to them [Adam and Eve] 'be fruitful and multiply, fill the earth and subdue it; and rule over the fish of the sea, the bird of the sky, and every living thing that moves on the earth[15]

The commentaries interpret these words for us:[16]

1. *Fill the earth,* meaning do not congregate in one location but disperse throughout the globe. Humankind's mission is not associated with one location; the whole world is meant to be the human kingdom. Humans are

thus one of the few species that can acclimatize and thrive in any part of the globe.

2. *Subdue the earth*, meaning conquer and master the land.

3. *Rule over*, meaning utilize ingenuity to rule over the animals, both to prevent some from entering the human domain, and to ensnare others and catch them to serve humankind.

In summary, behaviorally modern Homo sapiens received a soul spark that had a burning desire to leave where it was and go on to conquer every part of the globe. And the fossil record has shown that this is exactly what they did—they left Africa, and over tens of thousands of years they reached every corner of the world. Furthermore, they developed agriculture and domesticated animals.

There was another need that these soul sparks experienced when they began to be incarnated into anatomically modern humans. Each soul's spark incarnated into a body brought with it the need for that body to be clothed.

According to Genesis, Adam was naked until he sinned.[17] It was only when he and Eve realized they had sinned that "*the eyes of them both were opened, and they realized that they were naked; and they sewed together a fig leaf and made themselves aprons.*"[18] The soul sparks that shattered from Adam's soul and began to be incarnated into anatomically modern humans had experienced the awareness of nakedness and need for clothing while part of Adam. From this analysis we expect humans to begin to clothe themselves coincident with the appearance of behavioral modernity.

Use of clothing is an important modern behavior that contributed to the successful expansion of humans into higher latitudes and cold climates. There is little direct archaeological, fossil, or genetic evidence to estimate the appearance of clothing, since it is made of soft materials that are not preserved in the fossil record. However, clothing lice evolved from head louse ancestors once humans adopted clothing, thus dating the emergence of clothing lice provides an estimate of the time of origin of clothing use. It has been estimated, with a significant margin of error, that clothing lice diverged from head louse ancestors by about 83,000 year ago.[19] A more definitive estimate of the latest time for the emergence of clothing has been obtained by archaeologists identifying very early sewing needles of bone and ivory from about 32,000 years ago. These were found near Kostenki, Russia, in 1988.[20] Yet another estimate comes from awls and perforators made of bone, which are believed to have been used to pierce holes in clothing. These were dated to be about 77,000 years ago,[21] and were found in Blombos Cave, Republic of South Africa.

Finally, there is another seemingly inexplicable change coincident with the appearance of human behavioral modernity. We saw earlier that Adam's direct descendants lived to almost 1,000 years of age owing to the large rectifications they had to accomplish. What about us, the normal people? We also saw earlier that on average we need 70 years to accomplish our relatively smaller rectification task. However, this time span is variable. The Lubavitcher Rebbe[22] explains this idea as follows:

> ...if a person is blessed with long life, it is because the Almighty wants him or her to focus on the main aspects of their life, those aspects connected to their soul, to spiritual things. Through their developing this side of their lives [i.e., carrying out the rectification of the soul], there will automatically be an increase in activity in their physical life as well.

Shouldn't Homo sapiens with incarnated soul sparks live longer than earlier ones without human souls? They must - right?

Recent research shows that

> Grandparent-aged individuals became common relatively recently in human prehistory, and that this change came at about the same time as cultural shifts toward distinctly modern behaviors—including a dependence on sophisticated symbol-based communication of the kind that underpins art and language…. We do not know exactly what … allowed so many more of them to live to older age.[23]

Or do we?

We've now come right to the point after the fifth step of the sin, 5,773 years ago (as of 2013). We will complete the story in future chapters by tracking Adam's direct descendants from this point on through the events of the Flood and Tower of Babel. In the next chapter, we will pause to summarize all the Biblical information on Homo sapiens explored thus far, and compare what we glean with the scientific record.

---

[1] Genesis 1:26.

[2] Rabbi Meir Zlotowitz, Bereishis, *Genesis / A New Translation with a Commentary Anthologized from Talmudic Midrashic and Rabbinic Sources* (New York: Mesorah Publications, Ltd., 1977), p. 70 on Genesis 1:26.

[3] Rabbi Meir Zlotowitz, Bereishis, *Genesis / A New Translation with a Commentary Anthologized from Talmudic Midrashic and Rabbinic Sources* (New York: Mesorah Publications, Ltd., 1977), p. 70 on Genesis 1:26.

[4]   "Anatomy of the Creation-from the teachings of Rabbi Yitzchak Luria," translation and commentary Byavraham Sutton; *likutei torah (chumash haari, bereishit*, p. 6), www.chabad. org/kabbalah/article_cdo/aid/380529/jewish/Anatomy-of-the-Creation.htm

[5]   Rabbi Nissan D. Dubov, "The Key to Kabblah - Adam," Chabad-Lubavitch Media Center, 2001–2011, www.chabad.org /library/article_cdo/aid/361873/jewish/Adam.htm

[6]   Babylonian Talmud, Sanhedrin 38b.

[7]   Rabbi Yitzchak Ginsburgh, *What You Need to Know About Kabbalah* (New York, Dwelling Place Publishing Inc., 2006).

[8]   (i) Rabbi Nissan D. Dubov, "The Key to Kabblah - The Four Worlds," Chabad-Lubavitch Media Center, 2001–2011, www.chabad.org/library/article_cdo/aid/361902/jewish/The-Four-Worlds.htm

(ii) Yitzchak Ginsburgh, "From Essence to Actualization: The Secret of the Staff of Aaron," Gal Einai Publication Society, 2004. www.inner.org/audio/aid/E_023.htm

[9]   Yitzchak Ginsburgh, The Hebrew Letters- Channels of Creative Consciousness, (Jerusalem: Gal Einai Publications, 1990), p. 153.

[10]   Yitzchak Ginsburgh, The Hebrew Letters- Channels of Creative Consciousness, (Jerusalem: Gal Einai Publications, 1990), p. 79.

[11]   Yitzchak Ginsburgh, The Hebrew Letters- Channels of Creative Consciousness, (Jerusalem: Gal Einai Publications, 1990), p. 93.

[12]   Yitzchak Ginsburgh, The Hebrew Letters- Channels of Creative Consciousness, (Jerusalem: Gal Einai Publications, 1990), p. 79.

[13]   H. Moose, *In the Beginning, The Bible Unauthorized* (California: Thirty Seven Books, 2001), pp. 321–322.

[14]   One day is 24 hours times 60 minutes times 60 seconds or 86400 seconds. One day for God is 1000 of our years or 1000 times 365.25 of our days. Therefore 9.6 seconds for God is 9.6 divided by 86400 times 365250 or 40.58 of our days. Which are 40 days and 14 hours.

[15]   Genesis 1:28.

[16]   Rabbi Meir Zlotowitz, Bereishis, *Genesis / A New Translation with a Commentary Anthologized from Talmudic Midrashic and Rabbinic Sources* (New York: Mesorah Publications, Ltd., 1977), pp. 73–74 on Genesis 1:28.

[17]   Genesis 3:7.

[18]   Genesis 3:7.

[19]   Melissa A. Toups, Andrew Kitchen, Jessica E. Light and David L. Reed, "Origin of Clothing Lice Indicates Early Clothing Use by Anatomically Modern Humans in Africa," *Molecular Biology and Evolution*, Sep 7 2010, Vol. 28, Issue 1, pp. 29–32.

[20]   Hoffecker, J., Scott, J., "Excavations in Eastern Europe Reveal Ancient Human Lifestyles," *University of Colorado at Boulder News Archive*, March 21, 2002.

[21]   Mourre, V., Villa, P. and Henshilwood, C.S., "Early Use of Pressure Flaking on Lithic Artifacts at Blombos Cave, South Africa," *Science*, Vol. 330, n 6004, Oct 2010, pp. 659–662.

[22]   Shaul Yosef Leiter, "The Responsibility of Longevity," KabbalaOnline | Ascent of Safed, www.kabbalaonline.org/ kabbalah/article_cdo/aid/1400367/jewish/The-Responsibility-of-Longevity.htm

[23]   Rachel Caspari, "The Evolution of Grandparents," *Scientific American* 305 (2), August 2011, pp. 45–49.

Chapter 9

Homo Sapiens: The Biblical vs. the Scientific Account

Man (Midrash 1,500 years ago) - He stands upright; he speaks; he understands, and he sees. He eats and drinks, procreates, excretes, and dies.[1]

Homo sapiens (Dictionary.net) - the only surviving hominin; species to which modern man belongs; bipedal primate having language and ability to make and use complex tools.

Torah and science sources agree on the unique physical and mental characteristics of humans. Both agree on the timeline of human appearance, both for anatomically modern and behaviorally modern humans. They agree there is a strong anatomical and biological relation between humans and other primates. They agree on the timing for the human exodus from Africa to populate the world, and they may agree on the timing for the origin of clothing. All these agreements are verifiable by hard evidence obtained from the fossil record and genetic analysis—the "photo album" of our time on this planet.

Exactly on how and why humans, and in particular, behaviorally modern humans, came about, and why they left Africa when they did and go on to populate every corner of the earth, Torah and science sources do not agree on. But these areas of disagreement, unlike the areas of agreement, are not verifiable by any observable hard scientific evidence.

These disagreements remain in the realm of a well-supported and researched scientific theory of the origin of species and man, and well-documented spiritual scriptures passed down from Moses; with a few interpretations made by the author which are unsupported by official Biblical sources.

Table 9.1 summarizes what we have learned about Homo sapiens. References for what is described in the table have been provided in earlier chapters where this same material is described in greater detail.

Table 9.1 Homo Sapiens: Biblical and Scientific Views

Event	Bible derived view	Scientific view
Anatomically modern humans appear	Earliest appearance 200,000 years ago. Made in similar process to other animals and sharing many physical and biological features with other primates.	Earliest appearance about 200,000 years ago. Earliest fossils 195,000 years ago. Evolved via speciation from a chimpanzee-human common ancestor.
Behaviorally modern humans with spoken language appear	No earlier than 120,000 years ago and certainly by 63,000 years ago. Appeared as a result of Adam's soul sparks becoming available to be incarnated into anatomically modern humans	By 60,000 years ago, perhaps starting about 120,000 to 100,000 years ago. No consensus yet on why or exactly how.
Humans leave Africa for every corner of the world	By 63,000 years ago. Because the incarnated soul sparks from Adam had been commanded to populate the world.	By about 60,000 years ago. No consensus yet on why. Facilitated by climate change.
Humans: bipedal, with spoken language and ability to plan	Humans only species to possess divine components giving them these features.	Humans evolved to have these features. No scientific consensus as to why/how.

Event	Bible derived view	Scientific view
Humans clothed	Coinciding with behavioral modernity. Clothing came about owing to awareness of nakedness resulting from the sin.	Probably coinciding with behavioral modernity; hard evidence by 32,000 years ago.

Which is it, evolution from apes or devolution from Adam? Or is God a genetic engineer? That is to say, did He deliberately manipulate genes in an organism with the intent of making that organism better? Who guided the change from apes to anatomically modern humans before injecting Adam's soul fragments into them? Or...?

It's too early to decide. First, let us explore two other well-known yet difficult to reconcile events that complete the story of humanity: the Flood and Babel.

---

[1]   H. Freedman and M. Simon, Eds., Midrash Rabbah Genesis, Soccino Press, NY, 1985, VIII 11, p. 61.

Chapter 10

The Flood

The Genesis Flood: perhaps no other Biblical account is more controversial and perplexing.

A worldwide catastrophic event, survived by only eight people and pairs of all the land animals and birds, coexisting for a year in a wooden boat the size of the Titanic. How is it physically possible to have a flood of such extent? How could all the animals be gathered and saved in a wooden boat? And where is the scientific evidence for this event that occurred not so long ago? Some say it's just a story. But we have argued that the Biblical text is accurate, so what actually happened?

The purpose of this chapter is not to conduct an exhaustive investigation of the Flood, which would require an entire book of its own, but to work though the Biblical text and sources to address the above issues and a few more questions in order to understand how this event shaped human history. We will, as before, follow both the Biblical and scientific perspectives of the account.

So far we have seen that anatomically modern humans, and later, behaviorally modern humans, emanated as a result of Adam's sin. We have also seen that they left Africa and went on to settle in every corner of the world. The Bible then returns to the story of humanity beginning about 6,000 years ago. However, the Bible does not follow the regular Homo sapiens masses, but focuses on a different group of humans, namely Adam and his direct descendants, who as we have seen in Chapter 7 had different and larger souls with bigger missions requiring longer lifetimes than the masses of Homo sapiens. By

6,000 years ago, the world population numbered in the millions,[1] yet the Bible focuses primarily on Adam and the generations that came from him. Ten generations occur between Adam and Noah, the main protagonist of the Flood narrative. Because of their long lives, Noah was born only 126 years after Adam's death. After the Flood, Noah's contemporaries, with their larger souls, have perished. Nonetheless, Noah and his children who survived the Flood and whose descendants went on to disperse throughout the world after the incident of Babel had a profound effect on human history—both in culture and language. It is the effect they had on human history that we seek to understand and compare to the scientifically derived evidence obtained though studies involving primarily archeology and genetics. To accomplish this, we will first fully characterize the Flood in this chapter, and then examine the Biblical account of Babel in Chapter 11.

The Flood - Natural or Miraculous?

According to Biblical chronology, the Flood starts in the year 1656 after the six days of creation, or 2106 BCE, about 4,000 years ago. Was it a miraculous event or did it occur within what can be described as nature?

In Chapter 8, we explained that God has different names, and His various names refer to the different ways in which He reveals Himself in creation. Thus, to understand the Flood narrative, the first thing we must do is examine which names of God are used in it, and therefore, what power of God is being revealed or enacted during the Flood. Two names appear in the Flood narrative: God's essential name, and the name Elokim. God's essential name expresses His essence, and is therefore associated with merciful and miraculous acts.[2] God's name Elokim corresponds to His property of strict judgment. Elokim creates nature through the act of apparent withdrawal or contraction of God's infinite light.[3] Elokim can be translated as "Master of all forces"[4] and the "Godly spirit of Law and Order."[5] The use of Elokim indicates that the actions in the Biblical account are governed by strict law and order, and everything that occurred had to be based on natural cause and effect.

The parallel between Elokim and nature (ha Teva in Hebrew) is further emphasized by their numerical values. As we saw in Chapter 4, every Hebrew letter has a numerical value contributing to a total value for every word. Mystical tradition teaches that if two words have the same numerical value, they are related. Elokim and nature have the same numerical value of 86. Thus, we conclude that Elokim is the revelation of the supernatural, as God appears in nature. God is manifest through this name, Elokim, as the inner essence of nature and its laws,[6] and God appears hidden within nature when the name Elokim is used.

In the Flood account, the name Elokim is used to command Noah and to speak to him about the Flood and its impact. Thus, Elokim is the name that officiated in everything pertaining to the Flood and its destructive work. On the other hand, God's essential name is used when it comes to protecting and saving the ark and its inhabitants.[7] For example, the account says, *"God* [Elokim] *said to Noah, 'The end of all flesh has come...'"*[8] and *"then God* [YHWH] *said to Noah, 'Come to the ark, you and your household...'"*

Thus we conclude that the actual physical Flood that is carried out by Elokim, meaning God hidden within nature, should be explainable in scientific terms by known phenomena such as storms, river overflows, tsunamis. However, the survival of the ark and its inhabitants required divine intervention, and thus is not completely explainable by scientific theories.

Description of the Flood

The Genesis account of the Flood is about 1,500 words long. However, the commentaries and Midrashim provide significantly more information about what actually occurred. The chronology of the Flood, as understood by most commentaries, is shown in Table 10.1.[9]

Table 10.1 Flood Chronology

Day of Flood	Biblical Date 1656–7	Western Date 2106–5 BCE	Flood Event
0	17 Cheshvan	Oct 27	Flood begins
40	29 Kislev	Dec 8	40-day rain ends; torrents begin; ark floats
190	20 Iyar	May 6	150-day period of torrents ends
191	1 Sivan	May 7	Water begins to recede
207	17 Sivan	May 23	Ark rests on mountains of Ararat
250	1 Av	Jul 5	Mountaintops are visible
290	10 Elul	Aug 13	Raven sent out
296	16 Elul	Aug 19	Dove sent out
303	23 Elul	Aug 26	Dove returns with olive leaf
310	1 Tishrei	Sep 2	Dove does not return; earth begins to dry
365	27 Cheshvan	Oct 27	Earth completely dry

The Flood account begins with a 40-day period of rainfall. Then the waters become deep enough for the ark to float, and these waters remain for another 150 days! During these 150 days the sources agree that the rains continue but are intermittent, not steady, as during the first 40 days. After 150 days the waters begin to recede, with the land becoming completely dry by Day 365.

We turn to other texts to add color to the above chronology. In reading the text it is important to keep in mind that the term "earth" is sometimes read by us as the planet earth, or certainly the land surface of the world. However, the main Hebrew word "erets", translated as earth, has a multitude of meanings both global and local (see Table 10.3).

Below are highlights relating to the start of the Flood:[10]

1. And all the animals, and beasts, and fowls, were still there, and they surrounded the ark at every place, and the rain had not descended till seven days after.

2. And on that day, the Lord caused the whole earth to shake, and the sun darkened, and the foundations of the world raged, and the whole earth was moved violently, and the lightning flashed, and the thunder roared, and all the fountains in the earth were broken up, such as was not known to the inhabitants before.

3. And at the end of seven days, in the six hundredth year of the life of Noah, the waters of the Flood were upon the earth.

4. And all the fountains of the deep were broken up, and the windows of heaven were opened, and the rain was upon the earth forty days and forty nights.

5. And Noah and his household, and all the living creatures that were with him, came into the ark on account of the waters of the Flood, and the Lord shut him in.

6. And all the sons of men that were left upon the earth became exhausted through evil on account of the rain, for the waters were coming more violently

upon the earth, and the animals and beasts were still surrounding the ark.

Below are highlights relating to the actual Flood:

1. During the twelve-month duration of the Flood, the heavenly bodies did not operate in order. The inhabitants of the ark, therefore, could not tell from the sun or moon whether it was day or night.[11]

2. The ark floated securely like a ship on the ocean, while the world around it was transformed into a tremendous no-man's land of water.[12]

3. The rain from above, and all the wells and fountains of the earth below, opened up and poured forth boiling hot water.[13]

4. Only the fish survived.[14]

5. The corpses of all the people killed by the flood were washed down to Babylon [Iraq]. The area was therefore known as Shinar.... The bodies were completely dissolved... Not a single bone was left intact.[15]

6. Only after 150 days when the ark rested on a relatively low mountain in Ararat did Noah realize that the waters had receded to a significant extent. From that time on it was possible to see how 'the water level continued to decline' by looking at where it reached on the side of the ark. When it reached the bottom of the ark, the 'top of the mountain was visible' [Genesis 8:5].[16]

Note that during this period of 43 days (see Table 10.1) between the ark coming aground and the mountain tops being visible, the water dropped only 11 cubits[17] (the depth the ark was submerged), or about 8 meters.

More insights into the Flood are gleaned from the Genesis text and associated Midrashim relating to the ark itself:

1. God made Noah take wood for the ark from "the area of the Ararat Mountains. These are [in the east of Turkey] towards Baghdad."[18]

2. The ark was three hundred cubits long, fifty wide and thirty in height.[19] There is some dispute as to the length of a cubit. Estimates range from 18 inches to 28 inches, with the higher estimate being most likely.[20] Table 10.2 shows the probable dimensions of the ark as compared to other ships, and Figure 10.1 depicts a comparable modern cargo ship.

3. The ark was to be made with compartments.[21] The ark had three levels.[22] There are various opinions as to the structure of the ark. Each level was divided into compartments. One opinion says there were 120 compartments another says there were 300[23] and; the largest estimate is 366 compartments per level.[24]

4. Opinions differ on what resided in each level. One opinion holds that refuse was in the lower level, animals in the middle level, and humans, clean birds, and provisions in the upper level. This would indicate that there were 300 compartments for animals, and just fewer than 300 for birds. However Pirké Rabbi Eliezer contends that the animals were in the lowest level, birds in the second level, and humans and reptiles in the highest level. This allows for about 366

compartments for animals, 366 for birds, and 360 or so for reptiles (leaving a few for Noah's family).[25]

5. The ark rested on the mountains of Ararat meaning the range of Cordyane district east of Tigris, south of Armenia,[26] thought to be near the current city of Cizre (on the border of Turkey and Syria, 400 to 450m above sea level).[27]

6. It is these same mountains that were covered by 15 cubits of water[28] as described in Genesis 7.19: *"The waters strengthened very much upon the earth, all the high mountains which were under the heavens were covered."*

7. Noah took in the ark seven pair of every clean, meaning ritually pure for sacrifice, animal and bird; and one pair of the other animals (including reptiles) and birds.[29]

8. Elsewhere in the Torah,[30] the guidelines for recognizing clean animals are revealed. Lists of animals and birds are also provided, and although not intended to be complete, there are about 57 unclean animals, 38 unclean birds, 15 clean animals, and 18 clean birds. If for a moment we assume these were all the creatures the ark had to house, then using seven for each clean pair and one for each unclean pair, we get 163 pairs of animals and 134 pairs of birds.

Table 10.2 Dimensions - Ark vs. Other Ships

Ark (cubits)	Ark (meters: 18 inch cubit)	Ark (meters: 28 inch cubit)	Titanic (meters)	Asian class cargo ship (meters)	Adriana class cargo ship (meters)
Length 300	137	213	269	266	210
Width 50	23	35.5	28	32	30
Height 30	13.7	21.3	53	Depends on load	Depends on load

Figure 10.1 Modern Cargo Ship - Similar Size to Ark

Now that we have described the Flood, we are ready to examine whether it was local or global, and therefore to ascertain exactly what happened to humanity.

The Flood - Local or Global?

The Genesis text is normally read as characterizing a global event where all humanity perished, except Noah and his family. Many lines in the text point to this interpretation. For example: *"God said to Noah, 'The end of* all *flesh has come...'"*[31] or

"The waters strengthened very much upon the earth, all *the high mountains which were under the entire heavens were covered"*[32] or *"from man to animal to creeping thing and to the bird of the heavens: and they were blotted out from the earth"*[33] and so on.

However, in prior chapters we have seen that Adam and his descendants were very different from the rest of Homo sapiens. We have also seen that although Adam and his descendants were confined to the geographic region described in Genesis, which only included part of the Middle East, other Homo sapiens inhabited every corner of the globe. The thesis presented in this chapter is that the Flood primarily affected Adam's direct descendants—Noah and his Biblical contemporaries—the generation of the Flood, and it had only a minor effect on the rest of the inhabitants of the world. Thus, the Flood was a local event. Do sources support such an interpretation? Yes, according to the Biblical text to some extent, logical derivations based on the description of the Flood and explicit information contained in Midrashim.

Finally, as we shall see in the next section, scientific evidence in no way allows for a global flood. And, recall that as Elokim brings on the Flood we should be able to find a scientific explanation for it.

Midrash

We begin by exploring the direct descriptions of the extent of the Flood in the Midrashim. Midrash Rabbah explicitly states it was a local flood:

> *The deluge in the time of Noah was by no means the only flood with which this earth was visited. The first flood did its work of destruction as far as Jaffé [Jafo], and the one of Noah's days extended to Barbary.*[34]

Barbary is the western coastal region of North Africa—what is now Morocco, Algeria, Tunisia, and Libya.

Figure 10.2 is a map of North Africa, the Middle East, and parts of Asia.[35] The black areas are ocean; the white and gray areas are land. The gray represents the land that would be covered by water if a flood reached a height of 400 meters above sea level. A flood of 400 meters has been selected for illustration purposes and because, as we shall see throughout the rest of this chapter, it matches well with the description of the Genesis Flood. For example, sections of Barbary are clearly flooded at the 400 meter level, as the Midrash tells us they should be.

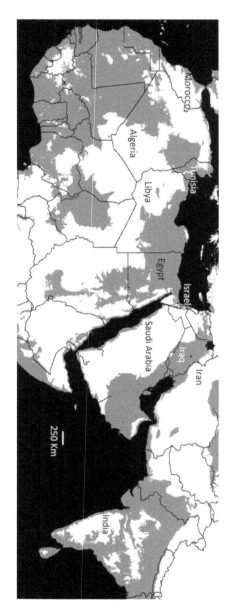

Figure 10.2 Flood of 400 Meter Depth

Jafo, where the first flood extended to, is on the Mediterranean coast just south of Tel Aviv in present-day Israel. What was this earlier flood? Another Midrash states:

> *These people had seen the troubles that their sins had caused. In the time of Enosh, the ocean had flooded the world twice, destroying two-thirds of the civilized world. Still they did not repent.*[36]

Yet another source indicates the following:

> *And every man made his god and ... forsook the Lord all the days of Enosh and his children; ...And the Lord caused the waters of the river Gihon to overwhelm them, and he destroyed and consumed them, and he destroyed the third part of the earth.*[37]

Enosh lived from 622 to 987. Noah lived from 1056 to 2006, and the Genesis Flood was in 1656. It is interesting to note the language: two-thirds of the world flooded, and the flood only extended to Jafo; one-third of the earth was destroyed by flooding the Gihon (recall this river is associated with Ethiopia only). Clearly, the world is not what we now consider planet Earth but refers to a much smaller region.

Finally, many sources state that Jerusalem was never flooded, and some state that the land of Israel was exempt from the Genesis Flood.[38] Yet, Jerusalem is only about 700 meters above sea level.

Derivation from the Description of the Flood

The description of the Flood provided above yields the following evidence for a local flood:

1. People killed by the Flood were washed down to Babylon (Iraq).

2. Geographically, this is the obvious place where the water from a local flood would drain to the Persian Gulf (see Figure 10.2).

3. The Ark started and ended in about the same geographic area. After the Flood, it rested on a relatively low mountain in Ararat. Its location is shown with a star in Figure 10.2.

4. Although we argue that the survival of the ark and its inhabitants had divine assistance, the ark still had to hold its inhabitants. The various interpretations of the size of the ark and number of compartments it contained allowed for hundreds of animals. Taking into account that the clean animals had to come in sevens, the ark could hold on the order of 100 animal species in total. There are millions of species in the world. An estimate of the order of 100 large animal species for the region described in Genesis is reasonable.[39] Thus, the ark was of the right size to save the local animal population but certainly could not accommodate the full animal kingdom.

The Biblical Text

The Biblical text provides many clues of a local, not global, event. Below are a few samples:

1. Psalm 104 is known as the creation Psalm because it parallels the Genesis creation narrative. The Psalm states: "*You set a boundary they* [the waters] *cannot cross; never again will they cover the earth.*"[40] Clearly, if the waters never again will cover the earth, then the Flood must have been local.

2. The term "earth," which appears numerous times in the Flood narrative is most often the translation of the Hebrew word "erets". Erets has both local and global meaning depending on context. (See Table 10.3) For example, in Genesis 11 (the Tower of Babel), the text says, "*the whole earth* [erets] *used the same language.*"[41] We know that this reference is not really to the earth at all (and certainly not to the "whole earth"), but to a group of people who all lived in one geographic location. It wasn't until later that God scattered the people "*over the face of the whole earth* [erets]"[42] (now presumably meaning the land surface of planet earth).[43] The word "adamah" is usually translated as ground, however sometimes it is translated as earth. Whereas erets is used in context of geography the word adamah relates to productivity. For example in Genesis 6.1 which says "*and it came to pass, when men began to multiply on the face of the earth* [adamah]*, and daughters were born unto them*" adamah clearly denotes productivity not geography; furthermore the geographic context is local.

3. In Genesis 8:5 we are told the tops of the mountains became visible, yet later in Genesis 8:9 we are told the dove returned because the water was still on the surface of the earth. But clearly part of the earth was dry if the mountains were already visible.

4. In Genesis 8:1–3 we are told that God remembered Noah, and the waters receded from the earth. But if it's a global flood, where do the waters recede to, and for that matter, where do they come from to create the Flood? The text is clearly speaking as if it were a local event where waters rise and recede from rivers and/or oceans.

In Genesis 8:13 we are told the earth was fully dried. This does not mean the planet earth was a desert with no lakes and rivers—it refers to the local land being dry as before the Flood.

Table 10.3 Meaning of the Hebrew Word "*Erets*"

Possible meanings	Possible interpretations
earth	• whole earth (as opposed to a part) • earth (as opposed to heaven) • earth (inhabitants)
land	• country, territory • district, region • tribal territory • piece of ground • land of Canaan, Israel • inhabitants of land • city
ground, surface of the earth	• ground • soil
in phrases	• people of the land • space or distance of country (in measurements of distance) • level or plain country • land of the living • end(s) of the earth
more recent usage	• lands, countries

Thus, we see that the text does not have to be interpreted to describe a global flood. In addition, logical reasoning based on the description of the Flood and other sources support a local flood.

Does Scientific Evidence Exist for the Flood?

There is absolutely no evidence for a global flood. The geologic record provides no worldwide clue of a flood. Straightforward calculations reveal that there is not enough water on the planet and in its atmosphere to cover all the land. In fact, 56 million years ago we have evidence that the earth was so warm that there was no ice on it. At that time the sea level was about 65 meters higher than now, covering only a small portion of the earth's surface.[44]

If there had been enough water for a global flood, then when the earth dried up, the atmosphere would have contained so much water vapor that we could not exist under its pressure.

Furthermore, as discussed in Appendix C, we have evidence that many cultures lived and survived during the period of the Genesis Flood.

What about a local flood? Most archaeologists and geologists recognize that there were indeed major floods that devastated substantial civilized areas. And many of the world's cultures past and present have preserved stories of a Great Flood that devastated earlier civilizations. In particular, there is plentiful evidence of local flooding in the region of the Euphrates and Tigris rivers.

Mechanisms to Produce the Flood within Nature

The description of the Genesis Flood is quite dramatic, certainly beyond anything we have experienced in recent history: darkened skies, boiling water, flooding hundreds of meters in depth, 40 days of rain.... Is there a "natural" mechanism for Elokim to carry this out? Perhaps.

The tools (within nature) available to Elokim to cause the Flood are described in Appendix C. These tools, like meteor impacts, earthquakes and tsunamis, can lead to prolonged periods of rainfall, release of ground water, flooding hundreds of meters deep, boiling hot water, obscuration of the sun and moon, even acid rain to dissolve materials—all these matching the catastrophic description of the Genesis Flood.

Nonetheless, it is hard to envision (although not impossible) how the Flood could have lasted so long. Figure 10.2 shows that there are no natural choke points to keep the flood waters from tsunamis, ground water release and rain on the continent for long; thus the waters would flow back out to the ocean in a relatively short period.

To explain how the ark floated for months after the initial rains and other events, we must assume that it spent a fair amount of time drifting in the Persian Gulf only to be brought back inland toward the end of the 130 day-period by a tsunami. In addition to explain the mountains been covered at least from Noah's vantage we would have to assume that the reason Noah could not see the mountains was not that they were covered by water, but obscured by fog and rain.

Impact of the Flood on Human History

Although the question of the extent and exact form of the Flood remains unresolved by our brief investigation, we can draw the key conclusions required for our purposes of understanding early human history.

1. The Flood was local, affecting only the Biblical area where the generation of the Flood lived, thus affecting primarily Adam's direct descendants, people with larger and special souls.

2. The rest of the surviving inhabitants elsewhere in the world (and animals and birds), although perhaps feeling some effects from tsunamis and rain, were largely unaffected. Thus, the Genesis Flood did not significantly affect Homo sapiens in general, nor their

cultures that became established all over the world after their migration out of Africa about 60,000 years ago.

3. Of Adam's direct descendants, only Noah and his family survived. As was the case with Adam, Noah and his family were commanded to *"be fruitful and multiply and fill the land."*[45]

It is Noah's children who we must now follow as they proceed to fill the earth, to understand their impact on human history. They formed a most important migration about 4,000 years ago and approximately 56,000 years after the first human migration Out of Africa. In the next chapter we shall study this migration from the Biblical and scientific points of view, in turn discovering how modern languages came to be.

---

[1]   (i) Colin McEvedy and Richard Jones, *Atlas of World Population History*, Puffin Books, London, 1978, pp. 342–351.
   (ii) For summary see U.S. Census Bureau www.census.gov/population/international/data/idb/worldhis.php

[2]   Rabbi Meir Zlotowitz, Bereishis, *Genesis / A New Translation with a Commentary Anthologized from Talmudic Midrashic and Rabbinic Sources* (New York: Mesorah Publications Ltd., 1977), p. 87 on Genesis 2:4.

[3]   Ibid.

[4]   Ramban on Genesis 1:3.

[5]   H. Moose, *In the Beginning: The Bible Unauthorized* (California: Thirty Seven Books, 2001), Genesis 1.

[6]   Yitzchak Ginsburgh, *The Mystery of Marriage* (Israel: Gal Einai Publication Society, 1999), p. 424.

[7]   H. Moose, *In the Beginning: The Bible Unauthorized* (California: Thirty Seven Books, 2001), pp. 320–326.

[8]   Genesis 6:13.

[9]   Rabbi Yaakov Culi, The Torah Anthology, (NY: Moznaim publishing corporation, 1988), p. 369.

[10]   *Sefer Ha Yashar, Book of Jasher,* translated (1840) from the original Hebrew into English (Salt Lake City: J.H. Parry & Company, 1887) Chapter 6.

[11]   *The Midrash Says, The Book of Beraishis,* selected and adapted from the Talmud and Midrash by Rabbi Moshe Weissman (Brooklyn, NY: Bnay Yakov Publications, 2006), pp. 94–96.

[12]   Ibid.

[13]   Ibid.

[14]   Ibid.

[15]   Rabbi Yaakov Culi, The Torah Anthology, (NY: Moznaim publishing corporation, 1988), pp. 370–371.

[16]   Mendel Weinbach, Reuven Subar, The Essential Malbim (New York: Mesorah Publications Ltd., 2009), p. 103.

[17]   Rabbi Meir Zlotowitz, Bereishis, *Genesis / A New Translation with a Commentary Anthologized from Talmudic Midrashic and Rabbinic Sources* (New York: Mesorah Publications Ltd., 1977), p. 262.

[18]   Rabbi Yaakov Culi, The Torah Anthology, (NY: Moznaim publishing corporation, 1988), p. 342.

[19]   Genesis 6:15.

[20]   Rabbi Yaakov Culi, *The Torah Anthology*, (NY: Moznaim publishing corporation, 1988), p. 342.

[21]   Genesis 6:14.

[22]   Genesis 6.16.

[23]   Rabbi Yaakov Culi, *The Torah Anthology*, (NY: Moznaim publishing corporation, 1988), pp. 342–3.

[24]   Michael Friedlander, *Pirkê de Rabbi Eliezer* [part of the oral law]. (Illinois: Varda Books, 2004), Chapter 13.

[25]   Ibid

[26]   Genesis Rabbah 33.4.

[27]   Rabbi Meir Zlotowitz, Bereishis, *Genesis / A New Translation with a Commentary Anthologized from Talmudic Midrashic and Rabbinic Sources* (New York: Mesorah Publications Ltd., 1977), p. 265.

[28]   Ibid

[29]   Genesis 6.

[30]   Leviticus:11:3; Deuteronomy:14:6; Deuteronomy:14:4–5; Leviticus:11:4–8

[31]   Genesis 6:13.

[32]   Genesis 7:19.

[33]   Genesis 7:23.

[34]   Midrash Genesis, Rabbah 23.

[35]   Produced by Dr. Ronald Caves using a digital elevation model of the world (GTOPO30 DEM).

[36]   Rabbi Yaakov Culi, The Torah Anthology, (NY: Moznaim publishing corporation, 1988), p. 326.

[37]   *Sefer Ha Yashar, Book of Jasher,* translated (1840) from the original Hebrew into English (Salt Lake City: J.H. Parry & Company, 1887) Chapter 6.

[38]   Michael Friedlander, *Pirkê de Rabbi Eliezer* [part of the oral law]. (Illinois: Varda Books, 2004), Chapter 23.

[39]   There are millions of species in the world. The region described in Genesis (first 10 chapters) is the home of a multitude of animal species from insects, to spiders and scorpions, to birds of prey, lizards, and deadly snakes. It is also the home of many mammal species, including rodents, wolves, hyenas, foxes, porcupines, baboons, gazelles, leopards, and

mountain goats. An estimate of the order of 100 large animal species for the region described in Genesis is reasonable. See Saudi Arabia - Plant and animal life, www.britannica.com/EBchecked/topic/525348/Saudi-Arabia/45201/Plant-and-animal-life

[40]   Psalm 104:9.

[41]   Genesis 11:1.

[42]   Genesis 11:8.

[43]   Genesis 11:6.

[44]   Robert Kunzig, "World Without Ice," *National Geographic*, p. 90–109 (October 2011).

[45]   Genesis 9:1; despite a translation as *"fill the land"* the words are identical to the blessing given to Adam in Genesis 1:28 where the phrase is translated as *"fill the earth."* The translation in annex A is also same for Genesis 9:1 and 1:28

Chapter 11

Babel

We have seen that as a result of Adam's sin his soul shattered, and the soul fragments became available to be incarnated into Homo sapiens. With these souls Homo sapiens became behaviorally modern, able to speak, and began migrating to every part of the earth. But what language did they speak? Adam spoke the language with which the world was created—Hebrew.[1] The Biblical sources don't tell us what these early behaviorally modern Homo sapiens spoke. Because they did not directly relate to or communicate with Adam, and only received minor fragments of his soul, we can surmise that they spoke initially a single language, presumably much more primitive than Hebrew. As they separated and migrated, the original language evolved into many different languages. These Homo sapiens developed cultures and languages in their different locations around the world for tens of thousands of years. Then, something remarkable happened about 4,000 years ago.

Adam and his direct descendants continued to speak Hebrew. So did the survivors of the Flood—Noah and his sons. Then 340 years after the Flood, in Babel, God confused their languages[2] and scattered them over the surface of the earth. We are told that 70 nations ensued, and as they spread they brought their culture and language to much of the rest of the world. This process began in the Biblical year 1996, or 1766 BCE, and continues to this day (as we discover new tribes in the Amazon, for example). We are most familiar with the episode of the European colonization of the Americas, typically dated to having started in 1492 CE, a period during which over many years Europeans brought their cultures and languages to America, infiltrating the original cultures established 14,000 years ago when the first migrations of Homo sapiens arrived on the American continents. However, according to Genesis, a similar process occurred elsewhere in the globe earlier in time as the 70 nations spread.

In this chapter we will return to the period at the end of the Flood and follow Noah's descendants to understand their impact on human history. We will then compare and contrast the scientific record with the Biblical record. At the end of the chapter we will be able to add a few more thousand years of early human history from Genesis and scientific studies to the history of Homo sapiens, from 200,000 years ago until 6,000 years ago, as summarized in Chapter 9.

So who were Noah's descendants? What were they like? Where did they go? What languages did they speak?

Noah's Descendants

Noah and his three sons (and their wives) emerged from the ark when the Flood had receded and the land was dry. We are told that "*God blessed Noah and his sons and He said to them, 'Be fruitful and multiply and fill the land* [earth].'"[3] Then we are told "*the sons of Noah who came out of the ark were Shem, Ham, Japheth - Ham being the father of Canaan. These three were the sons of Noah, and from these the whole world was spread out.*"[4] Thus, these three sons were not just individuals, but the progenitors of three types of people with different directions in life.[5] (As with the Flood we interpret "*the whole world*" to mean locally these people and their descendants and not include the rest of the Homo sapiens).

Noah's Three Sons

Each of the three sons was very different. The first hint of their differences can be derived from the order in which they entered the ark before the Flood. In Genesis 7:13 we are told that Shem, then Ham, and finally Japheth entered the ark. Shem, the youngest, was first, while Japheth, the oldest, entered last. This episode suggests their level of trust in God. Shem did not hesitate; his belief in God was solid. Ham needed an example to follow. Practical Japheth needed to evaluate all possibilities, and only when convinced the ark was the sole salvation did he enter.[6] We also know that no intercourse was allowed while on the ark, yet Ham disobeyed this rule.[7] Finally, we have a detailed account of how the three sons behaved during the incident of Noah's intoxication after he emerged from the ark.[8] In this account we learn that Ham observes the wrong in the incident and does nothing; Shem makes a moral judgment and takes action to fix the situation; and, Japheth sees Shem's view and is proactive in suggesting and carrying out a collaborative solution.

Based on the information provided for each son, the commentaries conclude the following:[9]

1. Shem exemplified someone with intellectual and spiritual goals;

2. Ham was a seeker of physical satisfaction whose animal desires made pleasure paramount;

3. Japheth was a practical-minded builder of nations governed by just man-made laws and rules.

Thus, we have the spiritual-minded son, the pleasure-oriented son, and the practical builder son. It was these three types who went on to found the new world.

The 70 Nations

As can be seen from the extensive list of descendants of Noah appearing in Genesis 10, Noah's three sons went on to have 70 descendants, each of whom became the ancestor of a nation:[10]

1. Japheth had 14 descendants (herein referred to by the numbers 1 to 14): *"from these the islands of the nations were separated in their lands - each according to its language, in their nations."*[11]

2. Ham had 30 descendants (referred to by numbers 15 to 44): *"these are the descendants of Ham, by their families, by their languages, in their lands, in their nations."*[12]

3. Shem had 26 (referred to as numbers 45 to 70): *"these are the descendants of Shem, by their families, by their languages, in their lands, in their nations."*[13]

The Dispersion of Babel

Three hundred and forty years after the Flood, all the descendants of Noah were together in Babel and speaking Hebrew.[14] From here their languages were confused, and they were dispersed.[15]

What languages did they speak after this event?

Where did they go?

We are not told what languages they spoke. However, the text *"by their families, by their languages, in their lands, in their nations"* makes it clear that each son's lineage was what we today describe as a language family or a group of related languages descended from a single ancestral language.[16] Nowadays we call the common ancestor language a "proto-language."

We do, however, have information as to where these nations of people went. By culling together written and oral Torah sources, rabbis have determined certain locations of the nations. Some locations remain under dispute, and others are simply not known. Figure 11.1 is a map of a portion of the world with current-day political boundaries showing the number of each nation plotted on its assumed location.[17] Missing numbers represent nations for which the location is not known or disputed; numbers with question marks beside them represent fairly certain locations; nonetheless, some uncertainty exists.

The pattern in Figure 11.1 is clear; the solid lines represent boundaries between the descendants of Noah's three sons. Based on the Biblical account, we expect to see language families along these boundaries emerge some 4,000 year ago, long after the original languages of the Homo sapiens.

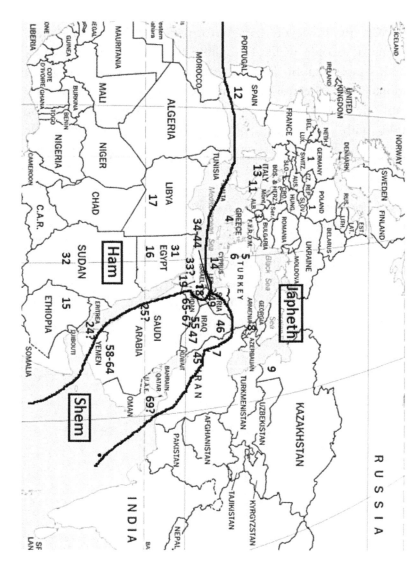

Figure 11.1 The 70 Nations

The Scientific Record on the History of Language

The study of language is a vast and complex field, perhaps one of the most challenging areas of scientific study today. This section provides only a glimpse of the subject and its findings. As was explained in Chapter 3, Homo sapiens began to speak most likely as they became behaviorally modern. Scientists today believe there was a first language, unlike any of today's languages, from which many thousands of languages evolved over time. Surprisingly, most of these are now extinct.[18] Although the origins of human language and the first language remain obscure, the source of individual languages has been the subject of very precise study over the past two centuries. Both genetic studies and linguistic studies are employed in the study of language.

Linguistically, the correlation of ancient languages is performed by seeking correspondences in grammar, syntax, vocabulary, and vocalization among known languages in order to reconstruct their immediate forebears, and ultimately, the original tongue. Living languages can be compared directly with one another; dead languages that have survived in written form can usually be vocalized by inference from internal linguistic evidence. Dead languages that have never been written, however, can be reconstructed only by comparing their descendants and by working backward according to the laws that govern the study of how word sounds change.[19] Nonetheless, even with the aid of genetic analysis, this is a difficult field, and many results remain inconclusive.[20]

There are perhaps 7,000[21] languages spoken in the world today; although 78% of the population speak the 85 largest languages.[22] Scholars group the languages into probably less than 20 families. Languages are linked to one other by shared words, sounds, or grammatical constructions. The theory is that the members of each linguistic group have descended from one language, a common ancestor. In many cases that original language is judged by experts to have been spoken in surprisingly recent times—in some cases as little as several thousand years ago.

The most widespread group of languages today is Indo-European,[23] spoken by just under half the world's population. This entire group, comprising languages ranging from Hindi and Persian to Norwegian and English, is believed to descend from the language of a tribe of nomads roaming the plains of eastern Europe and western Asia (centering on modern-day Ukraine). From about 2000 BCE, people speaking Indo-European languages began to spread throughout Europe, eventually reaching the Atlantic coast and the northern shores of the Mediterranean. They also penetrated far into Asia, occupying the Iranian plateau and much of India. A map[24] of the extent of this group around the time of Babel (1800 BCE) matches reasonably well with the extent of Japheth's family illustrated in Figure 11.1.

Another of the world's largest language families, with hundreds of living languages, is the Afro-asiatic language group, also known as Hamito-Semitic languages.[25] They are spoken by 200 to 300 million people primarily spread throughout the Arabian Peninsula, North Africa, and the Horn of Africa. These languages are believed to derive from the language of just one tribal group, possibly nomads in southern Arabia. By about 3000 BC, Semitic languages were spoken throughout a large tract of desert territory, from southern Arabia to the north of Syria. It is believed that these languages originated well before this date. The geographic extent of the language family matches remarkably well with Ham and Shem descendants in Figure 11.1. However, linguists believe these languages started much earlier than the Biblical Babel narrative suggests.

There are several other language families. The next largest is the Sino-Tibetan languages group,[26] a linguistic family comprising the Chinese and Tibeto-Burman languages, including some 250 languages of East Asia, Southeast Asia, and parts of South Asia. As languages are grouped into families, there are still some unclassified languages, although most of these are extinct.

Summary of the History of Language: Bible and Science

Certainly not all details are available to us regarding the history of language from either Biblical or scientific sources. However, there are no significant contradictions between the two bodies of knowledge.

Human language starts with behavioral modernity and evolves all over the world. About 4,000 years ago, the largest language family emerged near present-day Turkey/Ukraine and spread throughout Europe and parts of Asia where Japheth's descendants migrated. Another large language family exists where Ham and Shem roamed, although linguists believe these languages predate Babel. Many other language families exist that predate Babel and do not geographically coincide with the 70 nations' locations. These are clearly separate from the Babel migration (and the 70 nations) and originate from the much earlier Out of Africa migration.

As related in both the Biblical and scientific accounts, the spread of language is complex, encompassing tens of thousands of years. Today we know that many languages spoken in remote places are going extinct as they are no longer protected by natural boundaries or national borders from larger languages that dominate world commerce and communication. In a smaller scale this process has been going on for thousands of years.[27] It is not unreasonable that we can't completely reconstruct the language puzzle scientifically if the Biblical account described herein is accurate.

In summary, about 60,000 years ago, when Homo sapiens became behaviorally modern and began speaking, they developed thousands of languages as they migrated over the entire world. Then, only 4,000 years ago, a new worldwide migration ensued from Babel bringing with it 70 new languages. Languages interacted in perhaps three ways—as new migration met previously established peoples:

1. The more recent languages of the 70 nations overtook the pre-existing languages of Homo sapiens and became permanently established, as seems the case with Japheth's descendants and the Indo-European languages.

2. These newer languages mixed to some extent with pre-existing languages, as may be the case with Ham and Shem descendants and their Afro-asiatic language families.

3. The newer languages had no significant effect on earlier languages, and these earlier languages were able to continue evolving, as seems to be the case with language families like the Sino-Tibetan, and certainly with the indigenous languages of America (however, today these are threatened as processes 1 and 2 above continue).

It is fitting that the most unique human characteristic, language, which completes the early history of humans, remains elusive to our understanding.

[1]   Rabbi Meir Zlotowitz, Bereishis, *Genesis / A New Translation with a Commentary Anthologized from Talmudic Midrashic and Rabbinic Sources* (New York: Mesorah Publications Ltd., 1977), Rashi on Genesis 11:1, p. 333.

[2]   Genesis 11:7.

[3]   Genesis 9:1.

[4]   Genesis 9:18–19.

[5]   Mendel Weinbach, Reuven Subar, *The Essential Malbim* (New York: Mesorah Publications Ltd., 2009), p. 111.

[6]   H. Moose, *In the Beginning: The Bible Unauthorized* (California: Thirty Seven Books, 2001), Genesis 7:13, p. 323.

[7]   Babylonian Talmud, Sanhedrin 108b.

[8]   Rabbi Meir Zlotowitz, Bereishis, *Genesis / A New Translation with a Commentary Anthologized from Talmudic Midrashic and Rabbinic Sources* (New York: Mesorah Publications Ltd., 1977), Genesis 9:20–28 and commentaries.

[9]   Mendel Weinbach, Reuven Subar, *The Essential Malbim* (New York: Mesorah Publications Ltd., 2009), p. 111.

[10]   Genesis 10.

[11]   Genesis 10:5.

[12]   Genesis 10:20.

[13]   Genesis 10:31.

[14]   Rabbi Meir Zlotowitz, Bereishis, *Genesis / A New Translation with a Commentary Anthologized from Talmudic Midrashic and Rabbinic Sources* (New York: Mesorah Publications Ltd., 1977), Rashi on Genesis 11:1, p. 333.

[15]   Genesis 11.

[16]   *Merriam Webster Dictionary.*

[17] Rabbi Meir Zlotowitz, Bereishis, *Genesis / A New Translation with a Commentary Anthologized from Talmudic Midrashic and Rabbinic Sources* (New York: Mesorah Publications Ltd., 1977), Genesis 10, pp. 309–332.

[18] John McWhorter, *The Power of Babel*, (New York: Harper Collins, 2001).

[19] Ivanov, Vyacheslav V.; Gamkrelidze, Thomas, "The Early History of Indo-European Languages," *Scientific American* 262 (March 1990) pp. 110–116.

[20] Russell D. Gray and Quentin D. Atkinson, "Language-tree divergence times support the Anatolian theory of Indo-European origin," *Nature* 426 (27 Nov 2003) pp. 435–439.

[21] (i) Russ Rymer, "Vanishing Voices", *National Geographic*, V. 222, No 1 (July 2012), pp. 62.
(ii) John McWhorter, *The Power of Babel*, (New York: Harper Collins, 2001).

[22] Russ Rymer, "Vanishing Voices", *National Geographic*, V. 222, No 1 (July 2012), p 60–93.

[23] Ivanov, Vyacheslav V.; Gamkrelidze, Thomas, "The Early History of Indo-European Languages," *Scientific American* 262 (March 1990) pp. 110–116.

[24] "Map of Indo-European Migrations", indo-european-migrations.scienceontheweb.net/map_of_indo_european_migrations.html

[25] Kenneth Katzner, *The Languages of the World*, Third Edition (London and New York: Routeledge, 2002) p. 27.

[26] Kenneth Katzner, *The Languages of the World*, Third Edition (London and New York: Routeledge, 2002) p. 22.

[27] Russ Rymer, "Vanishing Voices", *National Geographic*, V. 222, No 1 (July 2012), pp. 62.

Chapter 12

Conclusions - Where to from Here?

Messiah, the Anointed One, the Great Peacemaker, and the Ultimate Leader, is a human being, the prophesied descendant of King David, who, thanks to his leadership ability and knowledge of Torah, will inspire the whole world to believe in one God and usher in an era of all human beings living together in peace and brotherhood—the messianic era.

When Adam and Eve ate from the Tree of Knowledge of Good and Evil, they created a mixture of good and evil in reality. Ever since, it has been up to their descendants to clarify the good from the evil. When this clarification process is finished, the Messiah may be born.[1]

How exactly are we to carry out this clarification process? And what does it matter, anyway? It seems like the affairs of humankind are predestined and divinely ordained. What choice do we really have?

The intersection of divine providence and free will is a major theological topic. The two concepts seem completely at odds: either everything is preordained and proceeding according to a plan or we have complete free will, right? Theologically, free will is absolute. We have free choice, and divine providence also is absolute, thus affairs will unfold according to His plan.

Contradictory? Yes.

Coexisting at the same time? Yes.

How is this possible?

Wave-Particle Duality[2]

The contradictory nature of free will and divine providence is reminiscent of quantum mechanics. In the early 1900s several amazing discoveries about nature were made. In the end it was concluded that everything exhibits wave and particle behaviors—yes, everything—light, subatomic particles, baseballs. A wave is spread out, has a frequency and speed, and travels. When waves meet other waves, they superimpose on each other. That means that the net amplitude caused by two waves, is the sum of the amplitudes which would have been produced by the individual waves separately. If two peaks coincide you get a much bigger peak, a process called constructive interference. When a peak and trough coincide, they cancel out each other and nothing is observed at that point, in other words it's dark; this is called destructive interference.

At first, light was thought to be a wave. Its wave behavior was most beautifully demonstrated by shining light of a single frequency through two vertical slits and observing the pattern on a screen (see Figure 12.1). Because the light behaves like a wave, the two slits generate waves that constructively interfere in some places causing light bands, while destructively interfering in others and causing dark areas. This pattern depends only on the light frequency, the separation of the slits and the width of the slits. Keep these the same, and you always get an identical pattern.

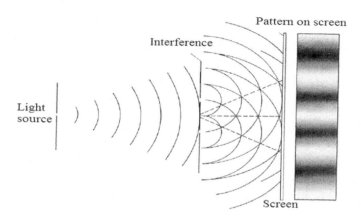

Figure 12.1 Two-slit Light Wave Interference

Now, light also behaves exactly like a particle (called a photon). You can shine light, one photon at a time, onto a surface and it will behave exactly as if a particle had hit the surface and collided with the particles there, perhaps dislodging some.

Experiment after experiment shows that light travels in the form of waves having frequency and wavelength and that exhibit interference effects, in addition to other effects. But light interacts, is emitted and absorbed, in the form of particles with discrete energies. This wave-particle duality has no easy explanation—light exists in both of these coinciding yet seemingly incompatible forms. Is this process beginning to sound like free will and divine providence?

Now here is the crunch. When light is sent one photon at a time through the two slits, as in Figure 12.1, each photon goes through and ends up on the screen. Where? We can't predict. It's as if each photon decided on its own and selected differently each time. However, after we shine a very large number of photons through and record where each lands, their totality forms a pattern, the same pattern of light and dark bands as in Figure 12.1.

Figure 12.2 illustrates the pattern on the screen as photons arrive; each panel represents the arrival of more and more photons. At first there is no pattern, but after numerous photons pass through, the pattern begins to emerge. That's right, each photon does make an unpredictable trip, but after some time they all achieve a predetermined, calculable pattern. We, the experimenters, have "divine foreknowledge" of the end result; we can achieve any pattern we want by changing the slit separation, width, and light frequency; yet each photon behaves individually as if it had "free will" (of course, actual free will applies only to humans).

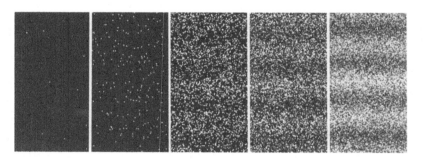

Figure 12.2 Pattern from Two-slit Interference

Thus, we see that nature provides a simple example of a phenomenon with a known pre-determinable outcome, in which each participant required to achieve that outcome exhibits unpredictable behavior. Furthermore, if the photons could look at each other as they approached the screen, they could not in their limited existence see the pattern. Rather, they would only see a few before and after them, and the places at which each arrived would seem random (see first two panels in Figure 12.2). Only we, the experimenters, watching the full timescale of the experiment see the pattern. So too do the last few "messianic" photons, for they see the final picture.

What do a bunch of photons have to do with the whole universe? A lot, as the latest physics is beginning to show. In some formulations of recent theoretical studies "the entire universe is described by a single quantum wave function, similar to the mathematical device that physicists routinely use to describe particles and atoms," including photons.[3]

Free Will and Divine Providence[4]

The Torah's teachings regarding free will and divine providence may be summarized as follows: as subjects, people act with unrestrained free will.[5] Our actions are voluntarily performed. Hence, we are entirely responsible for all our behaviors. As objects, however, people are governed by divine providence. How—if at all—we are affected by the voluntary actions of others is determined by divine providence. Hence, human responsibility notwithstanding, God is the true and only cause of everything that happens to us.[6]

Remember the story of Joseph and his brothers (Genesis 37–50)? When his brothers thought their father loved Joseph more than them, they began to hate their younger sibling. Then Joseph had a dream in which his brothers bowed down to him.

"Would you then reign over us?"[7] retorted the brothers.

Because of his dreams and words, they hated Joseph even more. His brothers became very jealous. They saw him in the distance and before he reached them, they began plotting to kill Joseph. *"Judah said to his brothers, What gain will there be if we kill our brother...let us sell him..."*[8] Thus, instead of killing Joseph, they decided to sell him into slavery in Egypt. At the climax of the story, when the brothers showed up in Egypt many years later, looking for food, Joseph said to them:

I am Joseph your brother - it is me, whom you sold into Egypt. And now be not distressed nor reproach yourselves for having sold me here, for it was to be a provider that God sent me here ahead of you. ... Thus God has sent me ahead of you to ensure your survival in the land and to sustain you ... and now it was not you who sent me here but God.[9]

Joseph reveals that the divine providence unfolded according to plan. He rose to second in command throughout Egypt and saved the entire region from starvation, as God had intended, for that is divine providence. Nonetheless, the brothers exercised their free will[10] to commit a sinful, punishable act. Free will existed; the brothers were liable for their bad behavior. All the same, the end results occur per God's predestined plan.

In a similar way, the photons follow their unpredictable path, but the final pattern still results according to the plan.

In summary, free will is granted to every human being. If a person desires to take the morally right path, he has the power to do so, and he rectifies his soul spark. However, a person is also at liberty to choose the morally wrong path and cause damage. This is a fundamental belief in the law and commandments: a person is judged according to his deeds. If he chooses the right moral action, he is rewarded; if he does evil, he will be punished.[11] On the other hand, divine providence is always at work; as the plan is divinely ordained.

Adam, His Free Will, and the Mission of Homo Sapiens

Adam could have obeyed the commandment to not eat the fruit, but he exercised his free will and disobeyed. As we have seen, the Divine plan must still unfold despite his act.

How?

Adam was given one great, all-inclusive soul, wherein it was difficult to discern the parts (the individual souls) because they were bound in singular unity. That was the Divine plan: a single, unified, rectified soul that could nullify itself and obey a "simple" command, one such as do not eat fruit from a particular tree for a mere three hours. When Adam sinned, his unified soul shattered into billions of soul sparks, each of these sparks damaged by his sin. Each soul spark was destined to be born in a different body, with its recognizable uniqueness and particular characteristics. Each person thus born with a soul spark, and possessing free will, can exercise this free will to rectify his own small soul spark of the great soul of Adam, of which it is a part. Through this rectification process, eventually all soul sparks will be repaired so they can all reunite again as one.[12]

The reason for existence and the mission of Homo sapiens thus is to fulfill the Divine plan by repairing all souls and returning them to the level of unity from which they all originated, but on a higher level (by returning to unity while retaining the special individuality they worked for and acquired). It is this soul rectification process and human journey that we have studied with the aid of the latest scientific evidence and Scripture.

Human History

We have seen that after the sin, early behaviorally modern Homo sapiens spread throughout the world. Adam's, direct descendants also spread throughout the world at a much later time, bringing with them modern languages. Each individual went forth with free will and a soul spark from Adam's original soul. What has been happening ever since is that these individuals have, by and large, been exercising their free will in such a way as to try and rectify Adam's sin, one little step and soul spark at a time. Some, Adam's direct descendants, had big souls and had the potential to do much rectification; others, the majority, have had "normal" souls and the potential to perform a tiny amount of rectification. Some, like the constructively interfering photons, work toward light and good to move the plan forward, while others work toward darkness and hold back the plan. But the Divine plan, the final pattern, is destined; it is forming one bit at a time, and when it is complete, the messianic era will arrive.

This is analogous to having a large tank full of pure water. Someone comes along and spills the water; the rest of us try to get all the water back in the tank. Some collect buckets (Adam's direct descendants with their major souls). Some get in the way and cause more small spills; others collect just one drop—perhaps our generation. None of us can see the level of the tank—we just deliver our drop into the tank. Then one day the last drop is delivered, and the tank is full. That is the history of humankind that we have reviewed—starting 60,000 or so years ago with behaviorally modern humans (Homo sapiens with human souls) until today.

But how far along are we? Are we almost done? Is the tank almost full? Or to put it another way, which panel in Figure 12.2 are we at? Can some of us see the emerging pattern yet?

How Many People Have Ever Lived and Will Live on Earth?

We don't really know how much work each person does toward the rectification mission. But let's make some very simple assumptions to get a notion of our progress toward the Divine plan. Let's assume that each person gets one soul spark, and each person rectifies that soul spark. How many soul sparks are to be rectified? As we saw in Chapter 6, the amount is 225 billion sparks!

Even though we can't peek into the "tank," we are good engineers and can make an educated guess.

So how many people have ever lived on earth?

Guesstimating the number of people ever born requires selecting population sizes for different points from antiquity to the present and applying assumed birth rates to each period, starting at the very, very beginning of human modernity, about 60,000 years ago.

To perform the calculation we need to know the pattern of population growth. Did it rise to a certain level and then fluctuate in response to famines and climate changes? Or did it grow at a constant rate from one point to another? We do not know the answers to these questions, although paleontologists have produced a variety of theories. We are left with making simple assumptions: a constant growth rate applied to each period up to modern times. What growth rate? One has to guess from available data. This simple and less-than-scientific approach yields an estimate of about 108 billion[13] births since the dawn of the human race.

Now, what is the situation for our own era in the early 21st century? Consider the following estimates made for the year 2011:[14]

- 135 million people were born.
- 57 million people died.
- The world population increased by 78 million people.

These figures yield an estimated annual growth rate of 1.1%.[15] In addition the world population in 2011 was about 7 billion.[16]

Once again a simple calculation,[17] assuming the population growth rate and the birth rate remain constant, shows that 131 billion people will be born between the end of 2011 and the year 6000 (2240 CE). Thus, all in all, 239 billion (108 plus 131 billion) will have lived by the year 6000 compared to the available soul sparks for rectification of 225 billion.

Indeed, we are right on track for the messianic era to commence on or before the year 6000.

The End

---

[1] Yitzchak Ginsburgh, "The Clarification of Evil, The Inner Meaning of *Tu B'Av*" (Gal Einai Publication Society, 1996–2011), www.inner.org/audio/aid/L_901.htm

[2] Benjamin Schumacher, *Quantum Mechanics: The Physics of the Microscopic World* (U.S.A. The Teaching Company, 2009), Parts 1 and 2

[3] Steven Carlip, "Quantum Gravity in Flatland" Scientific American 306(4), April 2012, pp. 40–47.

[4] Rabbi Mayer Twersky, "Free Will and Divine Providence" (The TorahWeb Foundation, 1999). www.torahweb.org/torah/1999/parsha/rtwe_vayigash.html

[5] There are exceptions to this under certain circumstances, but the norm is as described.

[6] There are exceptions to this under certain circumstances, but the norm is as described.

[7] Genesis 37:9.

[8] Genesis 37:26–27.

[9] Genesis 45:4–8.

[10] Minority opinions say free will is so strong that the brothers could have chosen to kill Joseph (instead of selling him). This would have required a reconfiguring of events to still end up with someone else in Egypt achieving the Divine plan.

[11] Rambam *Hilchot Teshuva* 5:1, 3, 4.

[12] (i) Rav Avraham Brandwein, "Gilgul Neshamot - Reincarnation of Souls," 5756, Jerusalem, Translation by Avraham Sutton. www.projectmind.org/exoteric/souls.html

(ii) Yitzchak Ginsburgh, "The Clarification of Evil, The Inner Meaning of *Tu B'Av*" (Gal Einai Publication Society, 1996–2011). www.inner.org/audio/aid/L_901.htm.

[13]   Carl Haub, "How Many People Have Ever Lived on Earth?" (Population Reference Bureau, 2011), www.prb.org/Articles/2002/HowManyPeopleHaveEverLived onEarth.aspx.

[14]   "UNFPA State of the World Population 2011," Barbara Crossette (lead reporter), EN-SWOP2011-FINAL.pdf, United Nations Population Fund, www.unfpa.org/swp/

[15]   U.S. Census Bureau, January 2010, www.census.gov/population/international/data/idb/worldpo pinfo.php

[16]   "UNFPA State of the World Population 2011," Barbara Crossette (lead reporter), EN-SWOP2011-FINAL.pdf, United Nations Population Fund, www.unfpa.org/swp/

[17]   To calculate the number of births in the next 228 years (until year 6000), one uses the geometric series summation formula with a growth rate and birth rate given $(1- 1.011^{228})/(1- 1.011) = 1010$. Multiply by the annual births of 130 million per year and obtain 131 billion.

Annex A

Genesis[1]

Genesis 1

[26] And God said, Let us make man in our image, after our likeness: and let them have dominion over the fish of the sea, and over the fowl of the air, and over the cattle, and over all the earth, and over every creeping thing that creepeth upon the earth.

[27] So God created man in his own image, in the image of God created he him; male and female created he them.

[28] And God blessed them, and God said unto them, Be fruitful, and multiply, and replenish the earth, and subdue it: and have dominion over the fish of the sea, and over the fowl of the air, and over every living thing that moveth upon the earth.

[29] And God said, Behold, I have given you every herb bearing seed, which is upon the face of all the earth, and every tree, in the which is the fruit of a tree yielding seed; to you it shall be for meat.

[30] And to every beast of the earth, and to every fowl of the air, and to everything that creepeth upon the earth, wherein there is life, I have given every green herb for meat: and it was so.

[31] And God saw everything that he had made, and, behold, it was very good. And the evening and the morning were the sixth day.

---

[1] *The Holy Bible, King James Version.* New York: Oxford Edition: 1769; King James Bible Online, 2008, www.kingjamesbibleonline.org/

Genesis 2

[1] Thus the heavens and the earth were finished, and all the host of them.

[2] And on the seventh day God ended his work which he had made; and he rested on the seventh day from all his work which he had made.

[3] And God blessed the seventh day, and sanctified it: because that in it he had rested from all his work which God created and made.

[4] These are the generations of the heavens and of the earth when they were created, in the day that the LORD[2] God made the earth and the heavens,

[5] And every plant of the field before it was in the earth, and every herb of the field before it grew: for the LORD God had not caused it to rain upon the earth, and there was not a man to till the ground.

[6] But there went up a mist from the earth, and watered the whole face of the ground.

[7] And the LORD God formed man of the dust of the ground, and breathed into his nostrils the breath of life; and man became a living soul.

[8] And the LORD God planted a garden eastward in Eden; and there he put the man whom he had formed.

[9] And out of the ground made the LORD God to grow every tree that is pleasant to the sight, and good for food; the tree of life also in the midst of the garden, and the tree of knowledge of good and evil.

[10] And a river went out of Eden to water the garden; and from thence it was parted, and became into four heads.

---

[2] All capital letters LORD indicate where the essential name for God, YHWH, appears in Hebrew texts.

11 The name of the first is Pison: that is it which compasseth the whole land of Havilah, where there is gold;

12 And the gold of that land is good: there is bdellium and the onyx stone.

13 And the name of the second river is Gihon: the same is it that compasseth the whole land of Ethiopia.

14 And the name of the third river is Hiddekel: that is it which goeth toward the east of Assyria. And the fourth river is Euphrates.

15 And the LORD God took the man, and put him into the garden of Eden to dress it and to keep it.

16 And the LORD God commanded the man, saying, Of every tree of the garden thou mayest freely eat:

17 But of the tree of the knowledge of good and evil, thou shalt not eat of it: for in the day that thou eatest thereof thou shalt surely die.

18 And the LORD God said, It is not good that the man should be alone; I will make him an help meet for him.

19 And out of the ground the LORD God formed every beast of the field, and every fowl of the air; and brought them unto Adam to see what he would call them: and whatsoever Adam called every living creature, that was the name thereof.

20 And Adam gave names to all cattle, and to the fowl of the air, and to every beast of the field; but for Adam there was not found an help meet for him.

21 And the LORD God caused a deep sleep to fall upon Adam, and he slept: and he took one of his ribs, and closed up the flesh instead thereof;

22 And the rib, which the LORD God had taken from man, made he a woman, and brought her unto the man.

²³ And Adam said, This is now bone of my bones, and flesh of my flesh: she shall be called Woman, because she was taken out of Man.

²⁴ Therefore shall a man leave his father and his mother, and shall cleave unto his wife: and they shall be one flesh.

²⁵ And they were both naked, the man and his wife, and were not ashamed.

Genesis 3

¹ Now the serpent was more subtile than any beast of the field which the LORD God had made. And he said unto the woman, Yea, hath God said, Ye shall not eat of every tree of the garden?

² And the woman said unto the serpent, We may eat of the fruit of the trees of the garden:

³ But of the fruit of the tree which is in the midst of the garden, God hath said, Ye shall not eat of it, neither shall ye touch it, lest ye die.

⁴ And the serpent said unto the woman, Ye shall not surely die:

⁵ For God doth know that in the day ye eat thereof, then your eyes shall be opened, and ye shall be as gods, knowing good and evil.

⁶ And when the woman saw that the tree was good for food, and that it was pleasant to the eyes, and a tree to be desired to make one wise, she took of the fruit thereof, and did eat, and gave also unto her husband with her; and he did eat.

⁷ And the eyes of them both were opened, and they knew that they were naked; and they sewed fig leaves together, and made themselves aprons.

⁸ And they heard the voice of the LORD God walking in the garden in the cool of the day: and Adam and his wife hid

themselves from the presence of the LORD God amongst the trees of the garden.

[9] And the LORD God called unto Adam, and said unto him, Where art thou?

[10] And he said, I heard thy voice in the garden, and I was afraid, because I was naked; and I hid myself.

[11] And he said, Who told thee that thou wast naked? Hast thou eaten of the tree, whereof I commanded thee that thou shouldest not eat?

[12] And the man said, The woman whom thou gavest to be with me, she gave me of the tree, and I did eat.

[13] And the LORD God said unto the woman, What is this that thou hast done? And the woman said, The serpent beguiled me, and I did eat.

[14] And the LORD God said unto the serpent, Because thou hast done this, thou art cursed above all cattle, and above every beast of the field; upon thy belly shalt thou go, and dust shalt thou eat all the days of thy life:

[15] And I will put enmity between thee and the woman, and between thy seed and her seed; it shall bruise thy head, and thou shalt bruise his heel.

[16] Unto the woman he said, I will greatly multiply thy sorrow and thy conception; in sorrow thou shalt bring forth children; and thy desire shall be to thy husband, and he shall rule over thee.

[17] And unto Adam he said, Because thou hast hearkened unto the voice of thy wife, and hast eaten of the tree, of which I commanded thee, saying, Thou shalt not eat of it: cursed is the ground for thy sake; in sorrow shalt thou eat of it all the days of thy life;

[18] Thorns also and thistles shall it bring forth to thee; and thou shalt eat the herb of the field;

[19] In the sweat of thy face shalt thou eat bread, till thou return unto the ground; for out of it wast thou taken: for dust thou art, and unto dust shalt thou return.

[20] And Adam called his wife's name Eve; because she was the mother of all living.

[21] Unto Adam also and to his wife did the LORD God make coats of skins, and clothed them.

[22] And the LORD God said, Behold, the man is become as one of us, to know good and evil: and now, lest he put forth his hand, and take also of the tree of life, and eat, and live forever:

[23] Therefore the LORD God sent him forth from the garden of Eden, to till the ground from whence he was taken.

[24] So he drove out the man; and he placed at the east of the garden of Eden Cherubims, and a flaming sword which turned every way, to keep the way of the tree of life.

Genesis 4

[1] And Adam knew Eve his wife; and she conceived, and bare Cain, and said, I have gotten a man from the LORD.

[2] And she again bare his brother Abel. And Abel was a keeper of sheep, but Cain was a tiller of the ground.

[8] And Cain talked with Abel his brother: and it came to pass, when they were in the field, that Cain rose up against Abel his brother, and slew him.

[9] And the LORD said unto Cain, Where [is][3] Abel thy brother? And he said, I know not: [Am] I my brother's keeper?

[10] And he said, What hast thou done? the voice of thy brother's blood crieth unto me from the ground.

---

[3] Words in [square brackets] are additions made by translators to complete the meaning.

[11] And now [art] thou cursed from the earth, which hath opened her mouth to receive thy brother's blood from thy hand;

[12] When thou tillest the ground, it shall not henceforth yield unto thee her strength; a fugitive and a vagabond shalt thou be in the earth.

[13] And Cain said unto the LORD, My punishment [is] greater than I can bear.

[14] Behold, thou hast driven me out this day from the face of the earth; and from thy face shall I be hid; and I shall be a fugitive and a vagabond in the earth; and it shall come to pass, [that] every one that findeth me shall slay me.

[15] And the LORD said unto him, Therefore whosoever slayeth Cain, vengeance shall be taken on him sevenfold. And the LORD set a mark upon Cain, lest any finding him should kill him.

[16] And Cain went out from the presence of the LORD, and dwelt in the land of Nod, on the east of Eden.

[17] And Cain knew his wife; and she conceived, and bare Enoch: and he builded a city, and called the name of the city, after the name of his son, Enoch.

Genesis 5

[1] This [is] the book of the generations of Adam. In the day that God created man, in the likeness of God made he him;

[2] Male and female created he them; and blessed them, and called their name Adam, in the day when they were created.

[3] And Adam lived an hundred and thirty years, and begat [a son] in his own likeness, after his image; and called his name Seth:

[4] And the days of Adam after he had begotten Seth were eight hundred years: and he begat sons and daughters:

5 And all the days that Adam lived were nine hundred and thirty years: and he died.

6 And Seth lived an hundred and five years, and begat Enos:

7 And Seth lived after he begat Enos eight hundred and seven years, and begat sons and daughters:

8 And all the days of Seth were nine hundred and twelve years: and he died.

9 And Enos lived ninety years, and begat Cainan:

32 And Noah was five hundred years old: and Noah begat Shem, Ham, and Japheth.

Genesis 6

9 These [are] the generations of Noah: Noah was a just man [and] perfect in his generations, [and] Noah walked with God.

10 And Noah begat three sons, Shem, Ham, and Japheth.

11 The earth also was corrupt before God, and the earth was filled with violence.

12 And God looked upon the earth, and, behold, it was corrupt; for all flesh had corrupted his way upon the earth.

13 And God said unto Noah, The end of all flesh is come before me; for the earth is filled with violence through them; and, behold, I will destroy them with the earth.

14 Make thee an ark of gopher wood; rooms shalt thou make in the ark, and shalt pitch it within and without with pitch.

15 And this [is the fashion] which thou shalt make it [of]: The length of the ark [shall be] three hundred cubits, the breadth of it fifty cubits, and the height of it thirty cubits.

16 A window shalt thou make to the ark, and in a cubit shalt thou finish it above; and the door of the ark shalt thou set in the side thereof; [with] lower, second, and third [stories] shalt thou make it.

[17] And, behold, I, even I, do bring a flood of waters upon the earth, to destroy all flesh, wherein [is] the breath of life, from under heaven; [and] everything that [is] in the earth shall die.

[18] But with thee will I establish my covenant; and thou shalt come into the ark, thou, and thy sons, and thy wife, and thy sons' wives with thee.

[19] And of every living thing of all flesh, two of every [sort] shalt thou bring into the ark, to keep [them] alive with thee; they shall be male and female.

[20] Of fowls after their kind, and of cattle after their kind, of every creeping thing of the earth after his kind, two of every [sort] shall come unto thee, to keep [them] alive.

[21] And take thou unto thee of all food that is eaten, and thou shalt gather [it] to thee; and it shall be for food for thee, and for them.

[22] Thus did Noah; according to all that God commanded him, so did he.

Genesis 7

[5] And Noah did according unto all that the LORD commanded him.

[6] And Noah [was] six hundred years old when the flood of waters was upon the earth.

[7] And Noah went in, and his sons, and his wife, and his sons' wives with him, into the ark, because of the waters of the flood.

[8] Of clean beasts, and of beasts that [are] not clean, and of fowls, and of everything that creepeth upon the earth,

[9] There went in two and two unto Noah into the ark, the male and the female, as God had commanded Noah.

[10] And it came to pass after seven days, that the waters of the flood were upon the earth.

11 In the six hundredth year of Noah's life, in the second month, the seventeenth day of the month, the same day were all the fountains of the great deep broken up, and the windows of heaven were opened.

12 And the rain was upon the earth forty days and forty nights.

13 In the self same day entered Noah, and Shem, and Ham, and Japheth, the sons of Noah, and Noah's wife, and the three wives of his sons with them, into the ark;

14 They, and every beast after his kind, and all the cattle after their kind, and every creeping thing that creepeth upon the earth after his kind, and every fowl after his kind, every bird of every sort.

15 And they went in unto Noah into the ark, two and two of all flesh, wherein [is] the breath of life.

16 And they that went in, went in male and female of all flesh, as God had commanded him: and the LORD shut him in.

17 And the flood was forty days upon the earth; and the waters increased, and bare up the ark, and it was lift[ed] up above the earth.

18 And the waters prevailed, and were increased greatly upon the earth; and the ark went upon the face of the waters.

19 And the waters prevailed exceedingly upon the earth; and all the high hills, that [were] under the whole heaven, were covered.

20 Fifteen cubits upward did the waters prevail; and the mountains were covered.

21 And all flesh died that moved upon the earth, both of fowl, and of cattle, and of beast, and of every creeping thing that creepeth upon the earth, and every man:

[22] All in whose nostrils [was] the breath of life, of all that [was] in the dry [land], died.

[23] And every living substance was destroyed which was upon the face of the ground, both man, and cattle, and the creeping things, and the fowl of the heaven; and they were destroyed from the earth: and Noah only remained [alive], and they that [were] with him in the ark.

[24] And the waters prevailed upon the earth an hundred and fifty days.

Genesis 8

[1] And God remembered Noah, and every living thing, and all the cattle that [was] with him in the ark: and God made a wind to pass over the earth, and the waters assuaged;

[2] The fountains also of the deep and the windows of heaven were stopped, and the rain from heaven was restrained;

[3] And the waters returned from off the earth continually: and after the end of the hundred and fifty days the waters were abated.

[4] And the ark rested in the seventh month, on the seventeenth day of the month, upon the mountains of Ararat.

[5] And the waters decreased continually until the tenth month: in the tenth [month], on the first [day] of the month, were the tops of the mountains seen.

[6] And it came to pass at the end of forty days, that Noah opened the window of the ark which he had made:

[7] And he sent forth a raven, which went forth to and fro, until the waters were dried up from off the earth.

[8] Also he sent forth a dove from him, to see if the waters were abated from off the face of the ground;

[9] But the dove found no rest for the sole of her foot, and she returned unto him into the ark, for the waters [were] on the

face of the whole earth: then he put forth his hand, and took her, and pulled her in unto him into the ark.

10   And he stayed yet other seven days; and again he sent forth the dove out of the ark;

11   And the dove came in to him in the evening; and, lo, in her mouth [was] an olive leaf pluckt off: so Noah knew that the waters were abated from off the earth.

12   And he stayed yet other seven days; and sent forth the dove; which returned not again unto him anymore.

13   And it came to pass in the six hundredth and first year, in the first [month], the first [day] of the month, the waters were dried up from off the earth: and Noah removed the covering of the ark, and looked, and, behold, the face of the ground was dry.

14   And in the second month, on the seven and twentieth day of the month, was the earth dried.

15   And God spake unto Noah, saying,

16   Go forth of the ark, thou, and thy wife, and thy sons, and thy sons' wives with thee.

17   Bring forth with thee every living thing that [is] with thee, of all flesh, [both] of fowl, and of cattle, and of every creeping thing that creepeth upon the earth; that they may breed abundantly in the earth, and be fruitful, and multiply upon the earth.

18   And Noah went forth, and his sons, and his wife, and his sons' wives with him:

19   Every beast, every creeping thing, and every fowl, [and] whatsoever creepeth upon the earth, after their kinds, went forth out of the ark.

20   And Noah builded an altar unto the LORD; and took of every clean beast, and of every clean fowl, and offered burnt offerings on the altar.

21 And the LORD smelled a sweet savor; and the LORD said in his heart, I will not again curse the ground any more for man's sake; for the imagination of man's heart [is] evil from his youth; neither will I again smite any more every thing living, as I have done.

22 While the earth remaineth, seedtime and harvest, and cold and heat, and summer and winter, and day and night shall not cease

Genesis 9

1 And God blessed Noah and his sons, and said unto them, Be fruitful, and multiply, and replenish the earth.

2 And the fear of you and the dread of you shall be upon every beast of the earth, and upon every fowl of the air, upon all that moveth [upon] the earth, and upon all the fishes of the sea; into your hand are they delivered.

3 Every moving thing that liveth shall be meat for you; even as the green herb have I given you all things.

4 But flesh with the life thereof, [which is] the blood thereof, shall ye not eat.

5 And surely your blood of your lives will I require; at the hand of every beast will I require it, and at the hand of man; at the hand of every man's brother will I require the life of man.

6 Whoso sheddeth man's blood, by man shall his blood be shed: for in the image of God made he man.

7 And you, be ye fruitful, and multiply; bring forth abundantly in the earth, and multiply therein.

8 And God spake unto Noah, and to his sons with him, saying,

9 And I, behold, I establish my covenant with you, and with your seed after you;

[10] And with every living creature that [is] with you, of the fowl, of the cattle, and of every beast of the earth with you; from all that go out of the ark, to every beast of the earth.

[11] And I will establish my covenant with you; neither shall all flesh be cut off any more by the waters of a flood; neither shall there any more be a flood to destroy the earth.

[12] And God said, This [is] the token of the covenant which I make between me and you and every living creature that [is] with you, for perpetual generations:

[13] I do set my bow in the cloud, and it shall be for a token of a covenant between me and the earth.

[14] And it shall come to pass, when I bring a cloud over the earth, that the bow shall be seen in the cloud:

[15] And I will remember my covenant, which [is] between me and you and every living creature of all flesh; and the waters shall no more become a flood to destroy all flesh.

[16] And the bow shall be in the cloud; and I will look upon it, that I may remember the everlasting covenant between God and every living creature of all flesh that [is] upon the earth.

[17] And God said unto Noah, This [is] the token of the covenant, which I have established between me and all flesh that [is] upon the earth.

[18] And the sons of Noah, that went forth of the ark, were Shem, and Ham, and Japheth: and Ham [is] the father of Canaan.

[19] These [are] the three sons of Noah: and of them was the whole earth overspread.

[20] And Noah began [to be] an husbandman, and he planted a vineyard:

[21] And he drank of the wine, and was drunken; and he was uncovered within his tent.

22 And Ham, the father of Canaan, saw the nakedness of his father, and told his two brethren without.

23 And Shem and Japheth took a garment, and laid [it] upon both their shoulders, and went backward, and covered the nakedness of their father; and their faces [were] backward, and they saw not their father's nakedness.

24 And Noah awoke from his wine, and knew what his younger son had done unto him.

25 And he said, Cursed [be] Canaan; a servant of servants shall he be unto his brethren.

26 And he said, Blessed [be] the LORD God of Shem; and Canaan shall be his servant.

27 God shall enlarge Japheth, and he shall dwell in the tents of Shem; and Canaan shall be his servant.

28 And Noah lived after the flood three hundred and fifty years.

29 And all the days of Noah were nine hundred and fifty years: and he died.

Genesis 10

1 Now these [are] the generations of the sons of Noah, Shem, Ham, and Japheth: and unto them were sons born after the flood.

2 The sons of Japheth; Gomer, and Magog, and Madai, and Javan, and Tubal, and Meshech, and Tiras.

3 And the sons of Gomer; Ashkenaz, and Riphath, and Togarmah.

4 And the sons of Javan; Elishah, and Tarshish, Kittim, and Dodanim.

5 By these were the isles of the Gentiles divided in their lands; every one after his tongue, after their families, in their nations.

[6] And the sons of Ham; Cush, and Mizraim, and Phut, and Canaan.

[7] And the sons of Cush; Seba, and Havilah, and Sabtah, and Raamah, and Sabtecha: and the sons of Raamah; Sheba, and Dedan.

[8] And Cush begat Nimrod: he began to be a mighty one in the earth.

[9] He was a mighty hunter before the LORD: wherefore it is said, Even as Nimrod the mighty hunter before the LORD.

[10] And the beginning of his kingdom was Babel, and Erech, and Accad, and Calneh, in the land of Shinar.

[11] Out of that land went forth Asshur, and builded Nineveh, and the city Rehoboth, and Calah,

[12] And Resen between Nineveh and Calah: the same [is] a great city.

[13] And Mizraim begat Ludim, and Anamim, and Lehabim, and Naphtuhim,

[14] And Pathrusim, and Casluhim, (out of whom came Philistim,) and Caphtorim.

[15] And Canaan begat Sidon his firstborn, and Heth,

[16] And the Jebusite, and the Amorite, and the Girgasite,

[17] And the Hivite, and the Arkite, and the Sinite,

[18] And the Arvadite, and the Zemarite, and the Hamathite: and afterward were the families of the Canaanites spread abroad.

[19] And the border of the Canaanites was from Sidon, as thou comest to Gerar, unto Gaza; as thou goest, unto Sodom, and Gomorrah, and Admah, and Zeboim, even unto Lasha.

[20] These [are] the sons of Ham, after their families, after their tongues, in their countries, [and] in their nations.

²¹ Unto Shem also, the father of all the children of Eber, the brother of Japheth the elder, even to him were [children] born.

²² The children of Shem; Elam, and Asshur, and Arphaxad, and Lud, and Aram.

²³ And the children of Aram; Uz, and Hul, and Gether, and Mash.

²⁴ And Arphaxad begat Salah; and Salah begat Eber.

²⁵ And unto Eber were born two sons: the name of one [was] Peleg; for in his days was the earth divided; and his brother's name [was] Joktan.

²⁶ And Joktan begat Almodad, and Sheleph, and Hazarmaveth, and Jerah,

²⁷ And Hadoram, and Uzal, and Diklah,

²⁸ And Obal, and Abimael, and Sheba,

²⁹ And Ophir, and Havilah, and Jobab: all these [were] the sons of Joktan.

³⁰ And their dwelling was from Mesha, as thou goest unto Sephar a mount of the east.

³¹ These [are] the sons of Shem, after their families, after their tongues, in their lands, after their nations.

³² These [are] the families of the sons of Noah, after their generations, in their nations: and by these were the nations divided in the earth after the flood.

Genesis 11

¹ And the whole earth was of one language, and of one speech.

² And it came to pass, as they journeyed from the east, that they found a plain in the land of Shinar; and they dwelt there.

³ And they said one to another, Go to, let us make brick, and burn them thoroughly. And they had brick for stone, and slime had they for morter.

4   And they said, Go to, let us build us a city and a tower, whose top [may reach] unto heaven; and let us make us a name, lest we be scattered abroad upon the face of the whole earth.

5   And the LORD came down to see the city and the tower, which the children of men builded.

6   And the LORD said, Behold, the people [is] one, and they have all one language; and this they begin to do: and now nothing will be restrained from them, which they have imagined to do.

7   Go to, let us go down, and there confound their language, that they may not understand one another's speech.

8   So the LORD scattered them abroad from thence upon the face of all the earth: and they left off to build the city.

9   Therefore is the name of it called Babel; because the LORD did there confound the language of all the earth: and from thence did the LORD scatter them abroad upon the face of all the earth.

Annex B

Divine Time

Divine Time is the fundamental inner working clock of the universe.

In this section we explore mystical works to arrive at an understanding of Divine Time and the relation between the Creation and Divine timelines. To determine Divine Time, one must first understand the central roles of numbers 7 and 49 in Biblical literature, and the concept of sabbatical cycles.

Cycles of 7 and 49

The numbers 7 and 49 are crucial in the Torah. Seven signifies completion of a fundamental process, e.g., the week. Forty-nine signifies the completion of seven cycles of seven, usually associated with more fundamental or final completion. These cycles involving 49 appear as complete spiritual, agricultural, and cosmic cycles. The first two are described in direct Biblical sources; the later cycles (cosmic) are derived from interpretation of a Talmudic source.

Spiritual Cycles - the Counting of the Omer

The Counting of the Omer is a verbal counting of each of the 49 days between the Jewish holidays of Passover, the holiday celebrating the exodus from Egypt, and Shavuot, the holiday celebrating the giving of the Torah. This commandment begins the day on which the Omer, a sacrifice containing an omer-measure (an ancient Hebrew measure corresponding to approximately 3.5 liters) of barley was

---

offered in the Temple in Jerusalem, and ends the day before an offering of wheat was brought to the Temple on Shavuot. The Counting of the Omer begins on the second day of Passover and ends the day before the holiday of Shavuot.

The commandment for counting the Omer is recorded in Leviticus:[1]

> *You shall count for yourselves—from the morrow of the rest day, from the day when you bring the omer of the waving—seven weeks, they shall be complete. Until the morrow of the seventh week you shall count, fifty days; and you shall offer a new meal-offering to God.*

The idea of counting each day represents spiritual preparation and anticipation for the receiving of the Torah. The period of the Omer is considered to be a time of potential inner growth, a time for one to further improve positive characteristics through reflection, and to further develop one trait on each of the 49 days.

Thus, spiritually, there are seven cycles of seven weeks with a complete spiritual cycle being 49 days.

Physical Cycles - Sabbatical Cycles for the Land

Shmita (literally release), also called the Sabbatical Year, is the seventh year of the seven-year agricultural cycle mandated by the Torah for the Land of Israel. During Shmita, the land is left to lie fallow and all agricultural activity—including plowing, planting, pruning, and harvesting—is forbidden by Torah law.[2]

> *For six years you may sow your field, and for six years you may prune your vineyard; and you may gather in its crops. But the seventh year shall be a complete rest for the land, a Sabbath for God…it shall be a year of rest for the land.*

The idea of the seventh rest year is also connected with debt. In the seventh year every creditor shall remit any debt owed by his neighbor and brother.[3]

> *At the end of seven years you shall institute a remission. This is the matter of the remission. Every creditor shall remit his authority over what he has lent to his fellow; he shall not press his fellow or his brother; for He has proclaimed a remission for God.*

After seven such sabbatical cycles, i.e., 49 years, comes the Jubilee, or the ultimate completion. The Jubilee year is the year at the end of seven cycles of Sabbatical years, and according to Torah regulations it had a special impact on land ownership and management in the territory of the kingdoms of Israel and of Judah.[4]

> *And you shall count for yourself seven cycles of sabbatical years, seven years seven times; the years of the seven cycles of sabbatical years shall be for you forty-nine years....You shall sanctify the fiftieth year and proclaim freedom throughout the land for all its inhabitants; it shall be the jubilee year for you; you shall return each man to his ancestral heritage and you shall return each man to his family.*

The Torah further states:[5] *"The land shall not be sold in perpetuity, for the land is Mine* [God's], *for you are sojourners and residents with Me."* The land can be sold only for the number of crops it will yield until the Jubilee year, when it reverts to its original owner. Thus, the Jubilee year existed because the land was the possession of God, and its current occupiers were merely tenants. Therefore, the land shouldn't be sold forever.

Cosmic Cycles - 49,000 Years[6]

One of the more controversial teachings is the doctrine of the Shmita applied cosmically.

Among the earlier generations of Kabbalists, prior to the Arizal, many wrote about the doctrine of the Shmita, including the Arizal's teacher, Rabbi David Ibn Zimra. They taught that not only is the doctrinal source of the Shmita to be found in the Oral Tradition, but also they made use of the plain words of the Torah text to show that the history of time is not fully told in the Torah alone.

As shown above, it is written in the book of Leviticus that for six years fields are to be sown, and for the seventh, the land is to be allowed to rest.[7] It is also taught by the Sages in the Talmud:[8] *"Six thousand years shall the world exist, and one [one thousand, the seventh], it shall be desolate."* Kabbalists learned from the secret meaning of the verse in Leviticus that the days of our world will be measured in the same way as the Biblical Sabbatical year. Six years shall we labor, and in the seventh shall we rest. So, our civilization will grow for 6,000 years, and then for 1,000 years shall it remain desolate, which means left alone to rest.

We are instructed to count seven times seven years and then to proclaim a Jubilee, a year of complete release. The Kabbalists have revealed that just as our civilization will last for the Sabbatical period of 6,000 years and 1,000 years of desolation, so will there be seven cycles similar to this, corresponding to a cosmic cycle of Sabbatical years totaling 49,000 years.

Thus, Biblical completion of spiritual and agricultural full cycles is 49 days and years respectively. Cosmically, the equivalent is 49,000 years, at which point the physical universe returns to its original owner.

The Divine Timeline

The concept of Divine Time and cosmic cycles has been developed and explained by Rabbi Aryeh Kaplan[9] and clarified by Rabbi Ari D. Kahn.[10] This section further develops the divine timeline and plots it in parallel to the creation timeline.

In the 13th century, Rabbi Isaac ben Samuel of Acre, in his work *Otzar HaChaim* (Life's Treasure),[11] agreed with the concept that the universe will exist for 49,000 years. His was the first work to teach that since Sabbatical cycles existed before man was created, time before Adam and Eve must be measured in divine years (where, as we saw earlier, one Divine day is 1,000 years of Human Time[12]). Rabbi Isaac ben Samuel of Acre was thus the first to see that the universe is billions of years old. Rabbi Aryeh Kaplan in his interpretation of Rabbi Isaac ben Samuel of Acre's work assumes that we are currently in the seventh sabbatical cycle. This is a controversial teaching, since most Kabbalists teach that we are in the second cycle.

The work described above has placed the occurrence of earlier cosmic cycles prior to the Genesis narrative. This author hypothesizes the following:

1. The cycles start with the beginning of the universe as we know it, with Day 1 in the Genesis narrative.

2. A creation day is an epoch of time.

3. The universe will exist for seven cycles, or 49,000 years.

4. The current cycle is the last 7,000-year cycle, or seventh cycle, as we approach the messianic era.

Therefore, each of the six creation days is 7,000 years, one cycle, and we are now in the last 7,000 years of the existence of the universe as we know it, or the seventh cycle.

The above result is inspired by the controversial concept of cosmic cycles. However, more recent works support the 7,000-years-per-creation-day approach and thus lead to the same result. Rabbi Isaac Luria, the Arizal, does not support the concept of cosmic sabbatical cycles. The book *Etz Chaim* is a classic of Rabbi Isaac Luria's School of Kabbalah. Rabbi Salman Eliyahu, in his book *Kerem Shlomo on Etz Chaim* (a commentary on Etz Chaim), asserts that if something is perfected and complete, it has gone through a whole 7,000-year cycle. Each of the creation days was perfected, rectified, and pure, and had gone through its own 7,000-year completion; thus, each creation day represents 7,000 years.[13]

Given the above, Divine Time proceeds in periods of 7,000 years. As illustrated in Table B.1 below, each of the first six days of creation corresponds to 7,000 divine years: Day 1, from 0 to 7,000; Day 2, from 7,000 to 14,000; and so on, until Day 6, from 35,000 to 42,000. Following Day 6, from year 42,000 to 49,000, Divine Time corresponds to the 6,000 years of the Jewish calendar followed by the 1,000 years of the seventh millennium.

Table B.1 Seven Sabbatical Cycles

Creation Time	Day 1	Day 2	Day 3	Day 4	Day 5	Day 6	7,000 years*
Sabbatical Cycle	1st Cycle	2nd Cycle	3rd Cycle	4th Cycle	5th Cycle	6th Cycle	7th Cycle
Divine Years	7,000	7,000	7,000	7,000	7,000	7,000	7,000
Divine Time	0– 7,000	7,000– 14,000	14,000– 21,000	21,000– 28,000	28,000– 35,000	35,000– 42,000	42,000– 49,000
*7,000 years = 6,000 years of the Biblical calendar + 1,000 years of the seventh millennium							

Figure B.1 depicts the creation timeline for Day 6 and the parallel divine timeline.

Divine Time (thousands of years)	Creation Time		Creation Events
		12	
38500			
38792	974 generations before Adam	1	Dust was gathered
39083		2	Dust kneaded into shapeless mess; Formation of complex life begins
39375		3	Adam's limbs shaped
39667		4	Soul infused into Adam
39958		5	Adam rose and stood on his feet
40250		6	Adam named the animals
40542		7	Eve was created
40833		8	Cain and Abel born. Garden is planted after man created.
41125		9	Adam and Eve are commanded to not eat from the Tree
41417		10	Adam and Eve sinned
41708		11	Adam and Eve were tried
42000		12	Adam and Eve were expelled from the Garden

(DAY 6 (hours))

Figure B.1 Creation Time and Divine Time - Day 6

The "Birth" of Adam in Divine Time

The Talmud states "nine hundred and seventy-four generations pressed themselves forward to be created before the world was created, but were not created: the Holy One, blessed be He, arose and planted them in every generation."[14] This is also derived from the verse "The word which He commanded to a thousand generations,"[15] which, according to Rashi, means that the Torah was given, not for 1,000 generations, but to the 1,000th generation. By subtracting from 1,000 the 26 generations between Adam and Moses (who was given the Torah), we likewise obtain 974.

The Torah either gives us exact time for a generation by spelling out the dates when people were born and died (as for the generations between Adam and Moses), or in the absence of details, assumes a generation is 40 years. This is most famously expressed as "The wrath of God burned against Israel and He made them wander in the Wilderness for forty years, until the end of the entire generation..."[16] To calculate the time in Divine Time from the beginning to the end of the intended 974th generation, one multiplies 974 by 40 to obtain 38,960 years. Converting this to the time on the creation timeline (dividing 38,960 by 7,000), we arrive at 1.577 hours into Day 6, i.e., 34.6 minutes into the second hour (see Figure B.1). This is the hour of which it is said, "God kneaded the dust into a shapeless mass," i.e., began to form Adam. This analysis shows that Adam was "born" precisely after the intended 974th generation, in the divine year 38,960, which further supports using 7,000 years per creation day to derive the divine timeline. (Please note that commentaries[17] on the Talmud verse quoted in the preceding paragraph place the intended 974 generations prior to Day 1, or prior to *"let there be light"*; thus, there is no commentary that justifies or supports the above calculation.)[18]

[1]   Leviticus 23:15–16.

[2]   Leviticus 25:3–5.

[3]   Deuteronomy 15:1–3.

[4]   Leviticus 25:8–13.

[5]   Leviticus 25:23 and commentary footnote.

[6]   Aryeh Kaplan, Yaakov Elman, and Israel ben Gedaliah Lipschutz, *Immortality, Resurrection, and the Age of the Universe: A Kabbalistic View* (Israel: Ktav Publishing House, Jan 1993), pp. 6–9.

[7]   Leviticus 25:3–5.

[8]   Babylonian Talmud, Sanhedrin 97a.

[9]   Rabbi Aryeh Kaplan, *The Age of the Universe: A Torah True Perspective* (Rueven Meir Caplan, 2008).

[10]   Rabbi Ari D. Kahn, *Explorations* (Israel: Targum Press, 2001), parshat Bahr.

[11]   Rabbi Isaac ben Samuel of Acre, *Otzar HaChaim (Life's Treasure)*, Guenz-berg collection, Lenin Library, Moscow. Also Rabbi Aryeh Kaplan, *The Age of the Universe: A Torah True Perspective* (Rueven Meir Caplan, 2008), p. 17.

[12]   *"For a thousand years in your sight are but like yesterday when it is past"* (Psalm 90:4), as interpreted in the Babylonian Talmud, Sanhedrin 97a and 97b.

[13]   Yitzchak Ginsburgh, *The Shemitot and the Age of the Universe*, Gal Einai Publication Society, February 2011, part 3.

[14]   Babylonian Talmud, Hagigah 13b, 14a.

[15]   Psalm 105:8.

[16]   Numbers 32:1.

[17]   Yitzchak Ginsburgh, *The Shemitot and the Age of the Universe*, Gal Einai Publication Society, February 2011, part 3.

[18] It is interesting to note that it took 3 hours to form Adam to the point when he receives his soul. Since Adam is the father of humankind, and it takes 40 weeks to form a baby during pregnancy, these 3 hours of Adam's formation parallel the 40 weeks of pregnancy. Thus, 34.6 minutes into the 3 hours equates to the 54th day of pregnancy. Counting from conception (as the Talmud does, rather than from the last menstrual cycle), the 34.6 minutes equate to the 40th day of pregnancy. The Talmud says an embryo is considered unformed for the first 40 days and cannot be regarded as a fetus until after the 40th day (Babylonian Talmud, Yebamoth 69b); similarly, Adam became the equivalent of a "fetus" halfway through the second hour, when his generation started.

Annex C

Flood Background

Natural Flood Mechanisms

The description of the Genesis Flood provided in Chapter 10 is quite dramatic, certainly beyond anything we have experienced in recent history: darkened skies, boiling water, flooding hundreds of meters in depth, 40 days of rain.... Is there a "natural" mechanism for Elokim to carry this out? Perhaps. If the whole story could be condensed into weeks, the answer would be a definite yes, but it's hard to envisage how a flood could endure so long. Let's explore the key mechanisms to cause the events and effects described in the Flood:

1. **Storms.** We are all familiar with heavy rainfall causing rivers to overflow and leading to extensive flooding. Can it rain for 40 days straight? In 1861 intense storms poured rain on California[1] for 43 days. Thousands of people and hundreds of thousands of animals died, whole communities were swept away, an inland sea of 300 miles by 20 miles formed and areas remained under water for six months.

2. **Volcanic eruptions.** Most of us have heard of the 1835 eruption of Krakatoa. This event illustrates the destruction that large volcanic eruptions can cause.[2] The combination of fast-moving currents of superheated gas (which can reach temperatures of about 1,000 °C) and rock, volcanic ashes (which darkened the skies for months), and tsunamis (the largest at 46 meters destroyed the town of Merak) had

disastrous results in the region. There were no survivors from 3,000 people located on an island about 13 km from Krakatoa. One thousand people were killed at town on the coast of Sumatra some 40 km north of Krakatoa. The official death toll recorded by the Dutch authorities was 36,417, although some sources put the estimate at 120,000 or more. Many settlements were destroyed. There are numerous documented reports of groups of human skeletons floating across the Indian Ocean on rafts of volcanic pumice and washing up on the east coast of Africa, up to a year after the eruption.

Although there are many land and submerged volcanoes near the scene of the Genesis Flood, no large eruptions from these have yet been dated that correspond with the time of the Flood.

3. **Meteorite impacts.** Best known for the extinction of dinosaurs, meteors can cause the most devastating effect on earth. Meteorites can impact land or oceans. Here we explore an ocean impact based on theoretical calculations.[3] A meteorite impact on the ocean would cause a large steam cloud by the sudden evaporation of the seawater. This water vapor would remain in the atmosphere for a long period and lead to prolonged rainfall. A giant tsunami would be generated.

For a 10 km-diameter object, the leading edge would hit the seafloor of the deep ocean basins before the top of the object had reached sea level. The tsunami from such an impact is estimated to produce waves from 1 to 3 km high. These waves would travel thousands of kilometers and still be several hundred meters high; they would easily flood the interior of continents. The surrounding water returning over the hot crater floor would be vaporized (a large enough impact will break through to the hot lithosphere and maybe the even hotter asthenosphere), sending more water vapor into the air as well as causing huge steam explosions that greatly compound the effect of the initial impact explosion. The steam blasts from the water at the crater site rushing back over the hot crater floor would also produce tsunamis following the initial impact tsunami, and crustal shifting as a result of the initial impact would produce other earthquakes and tsunamis—a complex train of tsunamis would be created. The tsunamis would carry very hot water from the impact.

To understand the power of such an event, consider that the kinetic energy of the falling object is converted into an explosion when the object hits the water, and then the ocean floor. The largest yield of a thermonuclear warhead is about 50–100 megatons of TNT (1,000 times larger than the bombs dropped on Japan). A 10-kilometer object produces an explosion of 60 million megatons of TNT. A 1-kilometer object produces a milder explosion of 60,000 megatons! Large amounts of nitrogen oxides would result from combining nitrogen and oxygen in the atmosphere due to the shock produced by the impact. These nitrogen oxides would combine with water in the atmosphere to produce nitric acid, which would fall back to the surface as acid rain, dissolving many substances.

Most astronomers doubt that any large meteorites have crashed into Earth in the past 10,000 years. However, a well-respected group of scientists known as the Holocene Impact Working Group[4] hypothesize that meteorite impacts on Earth are more common than previously supposed, and they have studied effects they believe were caused by a recent impact.[5]

At the southern end of Madagascar lie four enormous wedge-shaped sediment deposits, called "chevrons" that are composed of material from the ocean floor. Each covers twice the area of Manhattan, New York. On close inspection, the chevron deposits contain deep ocean microfossils that are fused with a medley of metals typically formed by cosmic impacts. Deposits from mega-tsunamis contain unusual rocks with marine oyster shells, which cannot be explained by wind erosion, storm waves, volcanoes, or other natural processes. The chevrons point toward the middle of the Indian Ocean where Burkle Crater, about 30-kilometers in diameter, lies 3,700 meters below the surface. Such a crater could only have been formed by a meteorite many kilometers in diameter. The impact from this meteorite would cause the effects described above. Given the distance from Burkle Crater to the Arabian Peninsula, the tsunami from it could produce 400m waves at the southern end of the Arabian Peninsula, and thus flood the continent at that level. Burkle Crater has not been accurately dated, but is thought to be about 4,000 to 5,000 years old, making it a good contributory candidate for the Genesis Flood and perhaps other flood legends in the area, e.g., the Indus valley in India.

4. **Ground water discharge.** Natural discharge of ground water often occurs at springs and seeps and can be triggered or increased by earthquakes,[6] certainly large ones as produced by the impact of a meteorite. The Flood narrative relates that the wells and fountains of the earth below (groundwater?) released water.

5. **Land subsidence.** There are three ways in which land, several thousand years ago, could have become lower in elevation leading to significant flooding.

The first cause is earthquakes. Recently the Geospatial Information Authority of Japan reported immediate subsidence caused by the 2011 Tōhoku earthquake. Several large areas subsided, some as much as 1.2 m.[7]

The second cause of subsidence is due to the removal of ground water.[8] As stated above, this can occur as a result of an earthquake.

Finally, ground can subside in karst terrains (which occur in the Arabian Peninsula).[9] A layer or layers of soluble bedrock, usually carbonate rock such as limestone or dolomite, can be dissolved by fluid flow creating voids below the surface; over which the land collapses.

The natural phenomena described above can lead to prolonged periods of rainfall, release of ground water, flooding hundreds of meters deep, boiling hot water, obscuration of the sun and moon, even acid rain to dissolve materials—all these matching the catastrophic description of the Genesis Flood. Nonetheless, it is hard to envision (although not impossible) how the Flood could have lasted so long.

Cultures Surviving the Flood

We have evidence that many cultures lived and survived during the period of the Genesis Flood. For example:

1. The Minoan civilization[10] on the island of Crete entered a cycle of cultural advancement about 2500 BC. These people had already produced works of art, established

cities, had an alphabet, and made use of bronze prior to the date of the Flood. It continued to develop and was established as a center of trade until it was destroyed by a volcano in 1470 BCE. Though this civilization was based on an island not far from the Middle East, there was no evidence of a flood in written or archaeological evidence.

2. The civilization of the Indus Valley[11] was a thriving state in 2500 BCE. It boasted two great cities. This civilization rivaled that of Egypt and Mesopotamia, and continued to exist uninterrupted until about 1500 BCE.

3. The Native Americans[12] and various tribes of Africa all survived the period of the Flood. There is no evidence that any of these millions of people suddenly disappeared from history and then suddenly reappeared all over the world practicing the same culture, art, language, and writing.

---

[1]   Michael D. Dettingerand B. Lynn Ingram, "The Coming Megafloods," *Scientific American*, January 2013, p. 66.

[2]   "1883 eruption of Krakatoa," en.wikipedia.org/wiki/ 1883_eruption_of_Krakatoa.

[3]   (i) Prof. Stephen A. Nelson, "Meteorites, Impacts, and Mass Extinction," Tulane University, 16 Nov 2011, www.tulane.edu/~sanelson/geol204/impacts.htm

(ii) Nick Strobel, *Astronomy Notes with CD* (3rd Revised edition), (Ontario: Irwin, 2004), www.astronomynotes.com/ solfluf/s5.htm

[4]   A group of scientists from Australia, France, Ireland, Russia and the USA who are established experts in geology, geophysics, geomorphology, tsunamis, tree rings, soil science and archaeology.

[5]   (i) Sandra Blakeslee, "Ancient Crash, Epic Wave," *New York Times news service*, Nov 14, 2006.

(ii) Scott Carney, "Did a Comet Cause the Great Flood?" *Discoverer magazine*, Nov 15 2007.

[6]   Michelle Sneed, Devin L. Galloway and William L. Cunningham, "Earthquakes - Rattling the Earth's Plumbing System," U.S. Geological Survey Fact Sheet 096–03, http://pubs.usgs.gov/fs/fs-096-03/.

[7]   "Land subsidence caused by 2011 Tōhoku earthquake and tsunami" (in Japanese). Geospatial Information Authority of Japan, 14 April 2011, http://www.gsi.go.jp/sokuchikijun/sokuchikijun40003.html.

[8]   Devin L. Galloway and Thomas J. Burbey, "Review: Regional land subsidence accompanying groundwater extraction," *Hydrogeology Journal*, 2011, v.19, pp. 1459–1486.

[9]   Ammar Amin and Khalid Bankher, "Causes of Land Subsidence in the Kingdom of Saudi Arabia," *Natural Hazards*, 1997, v.16. pp. 57–63.

[10]   "Minoan civilization," *Encyclopedia Britannica*. www.britannica.com/EBchecked/topic/384401/Minoan-civilization

[11]   "Indus Valley civilization (c. 2500–1800 BC)," *Encyclopedia Britannica*. www.britannica.com/EBchecked/topic/556016/South-Asian-arts/65286/Indus-Valley-civilization-c-2500-1800-bc

[12]   "Middle American Indian," *Encyclopedia Britannica*. www.britannica.com/EBchecked/topic/381104/Middle-American-Indian/57736/The-prehistoric-period

Glossary

A moment: the minimal period of time it takes man or God to do something - 9.6 seconds.

A priori: made before or without examination; not supported by factual study.

Adam: the first created man. He looked nothing like us. Only after his sin was he diminished, thereby becoming more like us. Normal humans are referred to as humankind. Adam is referred to as Adam or man.

Anatomically modern humans: early Homo sapiens appearing about 200,000 years ago; humans in anatomy but not in behavior.

Angel: a spiritual being without physical characteristics; a messenger sent by God to perform certain tasks (*malach* in Hebrew).

Animalistic soul: component of the soul that is mainly emotional, although it contains some intellect to aid understanding of what is good for it and to attain what it wants, e.g., health.

Arizal or Ari: Rabbi Isaac Luria (1534–1572 CE), considered the father of contemporary Kabbalah. His teachings are referred to as Lurianic Kabbalah, these describing new, coherent doctrines of the origins of Creation and its cosmic rectification, while incorporating a recasting and fuller systemization of preceding Kabbalistic teaching.

Babel: the city, probably in present-day Iraq, where the post-Flood generation built a tower, 340 years after the Flood, and were dispersed by God after He confused their languages. Babel in Hebrew is composed of two words meaning "confusion has come."

Behaviorally modern humans: Homo sapiens appearing by about 60,000 years ago and that exhibit modern behaviors such as language.

Behavioral modernity: name given to era wherein all groups of people are observed to share certain unique, higher-order behaviors. Examples include language, art, music, myth, and cooking. These developments are often thought to be associated with the origin of language.

BCE: before the Common Era.

Bipedal: using only two legs for purpose of walking upright.

Birth rate: the number of live births per thousand people in a population per year.

BY: billion years.

Cambrian explosion: the relatively rapid appearance of complex animals approximately 530 million years ago, as found in the fossil record.

Chimpanzee: a great ape with large ears, mainly black coloration, and lighter skin on the face. Native to the forests of western and central Africa, chimpanzees show advanced behaviors such as the making and using of tools

Christian right: a term used predominantly in the United States to describe a spectrum of right-wing Christian political and social movements and organizations characterized by strong support of conservative social and political values.

Chromosome: a structure within the cell that bears the genetic material as a threadlike linear strand of DNA.

Commentaries: critical explanations or interpretations of the Biblical texts.

Common ancestor: the most recent ancestral form or species from which two different species are thought to have evolved from. Also used in genealogy, to denote any person to whom two or more persons claim descent.

Cosmology: the study of how the universe began and developed.

Counting of the Omer: a verbal counting of each of the 49 days between the Jewish holidays of Passover (the holiday celebrating the exodus from Egypt) and Shavuot (the holiday celebrating the giving of the Torah).

Creation day: 2.54 billion years in Human Time, or 7,000 years in Divine Time.

Creation Time: time as per the six-day creation account in Genesis.

Creation timeline: the six-day chronological account of the creation of the universe and life in Genesis.

Creation: the divine act of making something out of nothing.

Creation-evolution controversy: also known as the origins debate; a recurring cultural, political, and theological dispute about the origins of the earth, humanity, life, and the universe. The dispute is among those who espouse religious belief and thus support a creationist view versus those who accept evolution as supported by scientific consensus.

Cretaceous Period: from 135 million to 63 million years ago; end of the age of reptiles; appearance of modern insects and flowering plants.

Cubit: an ancient unit of measurement, the cubit (from cubitum Latin for 'elbow') was the measurement from the elbow to the outstretched fingertip, which measurement varies from one person to the next. It was typically about 18 inches.

Divine day: 1,000 years of Human Time.

Divine providence: the notion that, despite human beings' possessing individual free will, affairs will unfold according to God's plan, i.e. the Divine plan.

Divine Time: time as kept by God. One divine day is 1,000 years in human terms (Human Time).

DNA: deoxyribonucleic acid, a self-replicating material present in nearly all living organisms as the main constituent of chromosomes. It is the carrier of genetic information.

Elokim: the name of God used in Genesis One, indicating that the actions in the creation account are governed by strict law and order, and everything that occurred had to be based on cause and effect.

Epoch interpretation: an interpretation of the six days in the creation narrative as six epochs or eras.

Eugenics: the study of hereditary improvement of the human race by controlled selective breeding.

Eve: the first woman. After she sinned, Adam called her Chavah, which means the mother of mortal life.

Extinction: the end of an organism or group of organisms, typically a species.

Extinction events: or mass extinctions; denotes large extinctions that have occurred over a relatively short period of time, during which the number of species that went extinct was significantly higher than that to be expected (five have occurred since life began).

Free will: the notion that humans have unconstrained ability to make moral choices.

Formation: the act of taking something that already exists and making it into something else.

Fossils: the preserved remains or traces of animals, plants, and other organisms from the remote past.

Genes: inside each cell, genes comprise a "blueprint" for protein production that determines how the cell will function. Genes also determine physical characteristics.

Genesis Flood: a large-scale flood described in Genesis that wiped out the direct descendants from Adam in the Biblical year 1656–7, equivalent to 2106–5 BCE.

Genetics: the branch of biology that deals with heredity, especially the mechanisms of hereditary transmission and the variation of inherited characteristics among similar or related organisms.

Genome: the entire genetic complement, all of the genetic information, all of the hereditary material possessed by an organism.

Genus: a taxonomic category ranking below a family and above a species, and generally consisting of a group of species.

Half-life: the time required for something to fall to half its initial value; in this work's context, the time for half the atoms in a radioactive substance to decay.

Ham: one of Noah's sons and a seeker of physical satisfaction whose animal desires made pleasure paramount.

Hominid: refers to humans, chimpanzees, gorillas, and their relatives. The term "hominoid" refers to living and fossil apes including chimpanzees, gorillas, gibbons, orangutans, and humans.

Hominin: a member of the human lineage, more closely related to living people than to chimpanzees or other living primates. This group was formerly called "hominids," but "hominid" is now used for referring to humans, chimpanzees, gorillas, and their relatives. The term "hominoid" refers to living and fossil apes including chimpanzees, gorillas, gibbons, orangutans, and humans.

Homo: genus that includes modern humans and species closely related to them.

Homo sapiens: the only surviving hominin and species to which modern man belongs; bipedal primate having language and ability to make and use complex tools; brain volume of at least 1,400 cc.

Human: see Homo sapiens.

Human Genome: the genome of Homo sapiens, which is stored on 23 chromosome pairs. Twenty-two of these are autosomal chromosome pairs, while the remaining pair is sex-determining. The human genome project was a 13-year endeavor, completed in 2003, that identified all of the 20,000 to 25,000 genes in human DNA and determined the sequences of the 3 billion chemical base pairs that make up human DNA.

Human Time: time as kept by human beings.

Hyoid bone: horseshoe-shaped bone situated in the neck that serves as an anchoring structure for the larynx. It is critical for speech production.

Incarnate: embody in human form. Past tense is incarnated.

Innate: possessed at birth (inborn); possessed as an essential characteristic (inherent); of or produced by the mind rather than learned through experience.

In the image of God: meaning with the power of understanding and intellect, with moral freedom and free will, and with the same creative process as God.

Intellectual soul: a component of the soul which is mainly rational and cerebral.

Intelligent design: the proposition that certain features of the universe and of living things are best explained by an intelligent cause, not an undirected process such as natural selection.

Intermediary: what exists between every two levels of reality. An intermediate is meant to unite the two levels, and thus shares characteristics of each.

Isaac ben Samuel of Acre (fl. 13th–14th centuries): a Kabbalist who lived in the Land of Israel; author of *Otzar HaChaim*.

Isotope: one of two or more atoms with the same atomic number (number of protons) but with different numbers of neutrons.

"It was good": phrase meaning "completed to the point that it was useful to man."

"It was so": phrase meaning "became eternally established."

Jane Goodall: Order of the British Empire (born Valerie Jane Morris-Goodall on 3 April 1934), a British primatologist, ethologist, anthropologist, and UN Messenger of Peace; considered to be the world's foremost expert on chimpanzees.

Japheth: one of Noah's sons. He was a practical-minded builder of nations governed by just man-made laws and rules.

Jubilee Year: the year at the end of seven cycles of Sabbatical years (see Shmita), which, according to Torah regulations, had a special impact on the ownership and management of land in the territory of the kingdoms of Israel and of Judah.

Kabbalah: receiving or tradition; a discipline and school of thought concerned with the mystical aspect of Judaism.

Kind: unit of life that is formed or created as described in Genesis; interpreted to correspond to a species.

Klipot: (lit. peel or shell) word used to describe coverings of impurity.

KY: thousand years.

KYA: thousand years ago.

Language family: a group of languages related through descent from a common ancestor, called the proto-language of that family. Membership of languages in the same language family is established by historical linguistics methods that compare languages to establish their relatedness.

Last universal ancestor: term for the hypothetical single-cellular organism or the single cell from which all organisms now living on earth descended.

Life: matter characterized by the ability to metabolize nutrients, grow, reproduce, and respond as well as adapt to environmental stimuli.

Lithosphere: the outer part of the earth consisting of the crust and upper mantle; approximately 100 km thick.

Louisiana Balanced Treatment Act: act passed in 1981 in the U.S. state of Louisiana that required schools to provide balanced treatment of creation and evolutionary science.

Lubavitcher Rebbe: Menachem Mendel Schneerson (April 5, 1902–June 12, 1994), a prominent Hasidic rabbi and the seventh and last Rebbe (Hasidic leader) of the Chabad-Lubavitch. Chabad-Lubavitch is a branch of Orthodox Judaism that promotes spirituality and joy through the popularization and internalization of Jewish mysticism as the fundamental aspects of the Jewish faith movement.

Ma: million years ago.

Maimonides: a pre-eminent Jewish philosopher and one of the greatest Torah scholars of the Middle Ages.

Messiah: a human being, the prophesied descendant of King David, who will inspire the whole world to believe in one God and usher in an era of all human beings living together in peace and brotherhood, that is, the messianic era.

Messianic age: an age where under the leadership of the Messiah the whole world will believe in one God and live together in peace and brotherhood; expected to start on or before the year 6000 or 2240 CE.

Meteorite: a stony or metallic mass of matter that falls to the earth's surface from outer space.

Mitochondrial DNA: DNA found in mitochondria and that contains some structural genes; is generally inherited only through the female line.

Midrash: meaning exposition; denotes non-legalistic teachings of the rabbis of the Talmudic era.

Midrash Rabbah: a Midrash dedicated to explaining the Five Books of Moses.

Modern Behaviors: term used to refer to a set of traits that distinguish present-day humans and their recent ancestors from both living primates and other extinct hominid lineages. Examples include language, art, music, myth, and cooking.

Modern Humans: our species, *Homo sapiens*.

MY: million years.

Names of God: different names that refer to various ways in which He reveals Himself in creation.

Nebular hypothesis: model explaining the formation and evolution of the solar system; a precursor of the Big Bang at the solar-system level.

Neo-Darwinian synthesis: maintains that evolution is a purely materialistic process driven by the natural selection of random variation at the genetic level.

Noah: the tenth and last of the antediluvian generation heads who was commanded to build an ark to save himself, his family, and the land animals and birds from the catastrophic Genesis Flood.

Noah's ark: a large wooden structure (perhaps the size of the Titanic), consisting of three levels and hundreds of compartments, where Noah, his family, the land animals, and birds survived the Genesis Flood over a period of one year.

Old earth creationism: umbrella term for a number of creationism concepts. The worldview of proponents is typically more compatible with mainstream scientific thought on the issues of geology, cosmology, and the age of the earth. Some proponents interpret the six days of creation as six epochs.

Omer: a sacrifice containing an omer-measure (ancient Hebrew measure corresponding to approximately 3.5 liters).

Oral Law: used to interpret and apply the Written Law. It is now documented in writing. It consists primarily of the Talmud, Explanations, Midrashim, and Zohar.

Organic evolution: the sequence of events involved in the evolutionary development of a species or related group of organisms.

Origins debate: see Creation-evolution controversy.

Otzar HaChaim: Kabbalistic work by Isaac ben Samuel. It was the first work to state that the universe is actually billions of years old; ben Samuel arrived at this conclusion by distinguishing between earthly "solar years" and "divine years," herein described as Human Time and Divine Time.

Out of Africa: or recent African origin hypothesis, which argues that Homo sapiens arose in Africa about 200,000 years ago and had developed modern behaviors and migrated out of the continent by approximately 60,000 years ago.

Paleontology: the study of past life forms as represented in the fossil record.

Phylum: a group of organisms with a certain degree of morphological or developmental similarity. Morphology includes aspects of the outward appearance (shape, structure, color, and pattern) as well as the form and structure of the internal parts like bones and organs. In the biological classification hierarchy, the phylum level has members numbering in the tens, whereas the more detailed species level has members numbering in the millions.

Pirkê De-Rabbi Eliezer ("Chapters of Rabbi Eliezer"): a Midrash that comprises ethical guidelines as well as astronomical discussions related to the Creation narrative.

Plate tectonics: a scientific theory that describes large scale motion of Earth's lithosphere.

Primate: mammal of an order that includes lemurs, bush babies, tarsiers, marmosets, monkeys, apes, and humans. Primates are distinguished by having hands, hand-like feet, and forward-facing eyes, and, with the exception of humans, are typically agile tree-dwellers.

Progressive creationists: a group that believes God intervened at various points in the geologic past to create the basic life forms that then evolved into the various species we know today.

Quantum Mechanics: the theory of mechanics that replaced classical mechanics (which is based on Newton's laws); is particularly useful in dealing with the mechanics of subatomic particles.

Radioactive dating: measurement of the amount of radioactive material that an object contains; used to estimate the age of the object.

Radiometric dating: see Radioactive dating.

Ramban: Nahmanides, also known as Rabbi Moses ben Nachman Girondi, Bonastrucça Porta, and by his acronym Ramban (Gerona, 1194–Land of Israel, 1270); a leading medieval scholar, rabbi, philosopher, physician and Biblical commentator.

Rank: see Taxonomy.

Rashi: Shlomo Yitzhaki (1040–1105 CE), better known by the acronym Rashi (RAbbi SHlomo Itzhaki); a medieval French rabbi famed as author of the first comprehensive commentary on the Talmud as well as a comprehensive commentary on the Written Law (including Genesis).

Science: the systematic process of gathering information about the world and organizing it into theories and laws that can be tested.

Scientific creationism: a branch of creationism that attempts to provide scientific support for the Genesis creation narrative in the Book of Genesis and disprove generally accepted scientific facts, theories, and scientific paradigms about the history of the earth, cosmology, and biological evolution.

Scientific method: a system of processes used to establish new or revised knowledge.

70 nations: the 70 descendants of Noah's three sons each of whom became the ancestor of a nation; based upon the ethnological table given in Genesis 10.

Shem: one of Noah's sons. He was the example of someone with intellectual and spiritual goals.

Shmita: literally "release"; also called the Sabbatical Year; the seventh year of the seven-year agricultural cycle mandated by the Torah for the Land of Israel.

Speciation: the evolutionary formation of new biological species, usually by the division of a single species into two or more genetically distinct ones.

Talmud: meaning instruction, learning; a central text of mainstream Judaism in the form of a record of rabbinic discussions pertaining to Jewish law, ethics, philosophy, customs, and history.

Taxonomy: in biology, the science of classification in hierarchical structure. Each level in the hierarchical order is called rank. At the top of the hierarchy is life, followed by several levels of further subdivision, culminating with the lowest level, that of species.

Theistic evolution: belief that accepts earthly species evolve, but insists God has a role in the process.

Tikkun: Hebrew for rectification.

Torah: consists of the Written Law and the Oral Law (see separate entry). The Written Law in turn consists of the Five Books of Moses, Prophets, Writings (or Psalms), Sanhedrin, Rabbinical Laws and Customs.

Trace fossils: marks left behind by an organism while alive, such as a footprint or feces.

Tsunami: series of water waves caused by the displacement of a large volume of ocean water. Tsunami waves do not resemble normal sea waves because their wavelength is far longer. Rather than appearing as a breaking wave, a tsunami may instead initially resemble a rapidly rising tide. Very large wave heights can be generated by events such as earthquakes, volcanic eruptions, and meteorite impacts.

Wave-particle duality: the idea that light can show wave and particle characteristics in different experiments. The idea extends to all matter as well.

Y chromosome: sex chromosome present only in males; DNA passed from father to son.

Young earth creationism: form of creationism that asserts the universe and life were created by direct acts of God during a relatively short period, sometime between 5,700 and 10,000 years ago.

Zohar: meaning splendor, radiance; the foundational work in the literature of Jewish mystical thought known as Kabbalah.

Index

Abel, 75, 76, 81, 97, 182, 201
abstract thinking, 40
Acre, Isaac ben Samuel of. *see* Isaac ben Samuel of Acre
Adam, 5–6, 10, 13–14, 55, 58–59, 85–101, 104, 133–134, 155, 167
formation
    birth of, 204
    creation of, 89–90, 114
    in Creation Time, 73–74
    creative process used by, 117
    definition of, 215
    descendants of, 106–107, 133–134, 173
    as divine being, 10, 94
    formation of, 89, 206n18
    free will of, 172–173
    height, 95
    human attributes, 90
    lifetime, 95
    as made in the image of God, 113–114
    moments, 120
    physical autonomy of, 116
    sin by, 92–97, 103–105, 120
    soul of, 96, 103–106, 173
"adamah," 147
Adney Sadeh, 108
Adni, 115
Adriana cargo ships, 139, 141
Africa. *see* "Out of Africa" or recent African origin hypothesis
Afro–asiatic language group, 162, 164
Akvah, 115
Alef, 55
American Protestants, 21
anatomically modern humans, 9, 40, 44, 104, 120, 122–123, 130, 133,
    215
angels, 68, 74, 85, 90, 215
animals, 20, 24, 30, 33–36, 44, 76, 81, 89–91, 96, 105, 108–109, 123,
    130, 133, 137–140, 146, 150, 203, 207, 216, 219
animalistic soul, 95–96, 215

apes, 9, 19–21, 35, 38–39, 43, 45, 91, 107, 109, 131
Apostle Paul, 7
Arabian Peninsula, 86–87, 89, 162
Ardipithecus, 43
Ari or Arizal. *see* Luria, Rabbi Isaac
ark, 118, 135–141, 146, 150, 156–157, 186–192, 224
Asian cargo ships, 139, 141
Australopithecines, 9, 39, 45

Babel, 6, 14, 125, 131, 134, 147, 155, 158, 162–164, 194, 196 , 215
Babylonian Talmud, 58–59, 63, 206n18
behavior
    modern, 40–41, 216
    symbolic, 40
Bible, 5, 7, 10–11, 22, 53, 55, 64, 71, 105, 115, 118–119, 130, 133–
    134, 163. *see also* scriptures; specific books
    as collection of ancient myths and fables, 5
    interpreting, 25, 53–68
    King James Version, 5, 177–194
    time in, 11–12, 58, 116
    view of Homo sapiens, 127–129
Biblical sources, 54, 56, 59, 107, 130, 155, 197
Big Bang theory, 11, 78
books of the Law (Pentateuch), 5

Cain, 75–76, 81, 97, 104–105, 184–186, 203
Cambrian explosion, 24, 34, 216
cargo ships, 139, 141
Catholic Church, 9–10, 17, 23
Chabad–Lubavitch, 223
Chavah, 93
Chayah, 93
Chidekel river, 87
chimpanzees, 2, 4, 9, 20, 29, 37–39, 45, 91, 107, 109, 130, 216, 219
Chomsky, Noam, 46
Christianity, 2, 6, 22
Christian right, 22, 216
Christians, x, 5, 7, 9, 24
chromosomes, 36–37, 216, 220, 228
chronology. *see* timelines
clothing, 42, 123–124, 129, 131

commentaries, 7, 53, 57, 59–60, 62–67, 71, 86, 94, 113, 122, 136, 157, 202, 204, 217, 226
conscious observer, 11–12, 77–79, 105
consensus theory of evolution, 22
continents, 9, 40, 42, 87–88, 150, 156, 208, 210, 225
cosmic cycles, 197, 199–201
cosmology, 17, 65, 217, 224, 227
Council of Europe, 25
counting of the Omer, 197–198, 215
creation, 89
    beliefs in America, 26
    Day 6, 10–11
    definition of, 215
    of humans, 1–2, 5–6
    steps, 115–117
    of universe and life, 1–2, 5–6
    of world, 8
Creation day, 71–73, 77–78, 201–202, 204, 215
creation–evolution controversy, 2, 17, 215
creationism, 18, 21–25
    beliefs in America, 26
    old earth, 18, 25, 27n8, 224
    progressive, 225
    scientific, 22–23, 25, 226
    young earth, 25, 27n9, 228
Creation narrative, x, 13, 30, 54, 57, 64, 80, 113, 146, 218
Creation Time, 57, 67–68, 72–79, 81, 105, 120–121, 202–203, 215
    conversion to Human Time from, 67–68, 78–79
    Day 6, 74–76, 81, 203
    moments, 120
    sabbatical cycles, 202
Cretaceous Period, 34, 217
cubits, 94–95, 139–141, 186, 188, 215
cycles
    cosmic, 199–200
    physical, 198–199
    sabbatical, 198–199, 202
    of 7 and 49, 197–200
    spiritual, 197–198

Darwin, Charles, 1, 9, 18–24, 107

dating, radioactive, 31–32, 224
David, 7, 165, 221
Day 6, 1, 10, 12–13, 58, 73–76, 79–81, 83n11–12, 106, 200–202,
    229–230, 239
day, 10, 11, 94, 118, 125n14
de Buffon, Comte, 20
de Leon, Moses, 66–67
de Sales, Delisle, 20
Deuteronomy, 5, 116–117,
divine day, 77, 117, 216
divine foreknowledge, 168
Divine plan, 103–104, 170–172, 174n10, 216
divine providence, 165–167, 169–170
Divine Time, 13, 68, 72–73, 77, 81, 112, 119–120, 195, 198, 200–202,
    215–216
    conversion to Human Time from, 13, 77
    Day 6, 12, 81, 201
divine years, 68, 77, 199, 200, 202. see Divine Time
DNA (deoxyribonucleic acid), 30, 36–38, 107, 214, 216, 221, 226

earth, 1–2, 4, 6, 12, 14, 17–18, 21, 23, 25, 27, 29, 31–34, 37, 55, 60,
    65, 71–74, 79–80, 85, 87,94, 104, 120–121, 127, 134–136, 138, 140,
    143–147, 149, 152–154, 172, 177–194
    appearance of life on, 1, 29, 34–35, 80
    old earth, 18, 31
    old earth creationism, 25, 27n8, 222
    young earth creationism, 25, 27n9, 226
"earth" ("erets"), 135, 145
Eden, 5–6, 75, 79, 85–86, 94, 114, 178–183
Egypt, 25, 66, 71, 86–87, 169–170, 174n10, 195, 210
Ehevi: name of God, 113
Ekyeh: name of God, 113
Elders, 57
Eliezer, Rabbi, 59–61, 137, 223
    Chapters of. see Pirkê de Rabbi Eliezer, 60–61
Eliyahu, Rabbi Salman, 200
Elokah: name of God, 113
Elokim: name of God, 113, 132–133, 140, 147, 205, 216
end time, 78, 83n11
Enosh, 143
epoch interpretation, 216

"erets" ("earth"), 135, 145
Ethiopia, 49n17, 86–87, 89, 143
Etz Chaim, 200
Euphrates river, 86–87
Europe, 19, 25, 40, 98n14, 160–161
Eve, 5–6, 10, 59, 61, 74–76, 79, 81, 92–97, 120–121, 165, 199, 201, 206
evidence of life, 31
evolution, 2–3, 9–10, 13, 17–26, 29, 39, 53, 91, 109, 129, 215, 220, 222, 224, 225
    beliefs in America, 26
    Catholic Church on, 9–10, 17, 23
    consensus theory of, 22
    creation–evolution controversy, 2, 17, 215
    Darwinian natural selection, 1
    Darwin's theory of, 18–19, 24
    human, 9–10, 13, 20–21, 39, 108
    micro–evolution, 24
    organic, 24, 222
    theistic, 23, 26–27, 225
exodus, 12, 57, 127, 195
explanations, 56–57, 60, 62–67
extinction events, 2, 18, 34–35, 206, 216

Five Books of Moses, 5–7, 15n5, 59, 63–65, 96, 221
Flood, 14, 22, 27, 32, 60, 105–107, 116–118, 123, 129, 131–149, 153–156, 205–210, 213, 217, 222
    chronology of, 132–135
    cultures surviving, 147, 149, 209–210
    highlights, 135–136
    as local or global, 135, 139–148
    location of, 144
    mechanisms of, 147–149, 205–209
    as natural or miraculous, 132–133
    scientific evidence for, 131, 140, 147–148
formation, 18, 30, 32, 76, 79, 81, 87, 89, 99n15, 201, 204n18, 217
40–day periods, 116, 134
49: cycles of, 195–197
fossil record, 1, 4,13, 19, 24, 29–35, 37, 45, 77, 80, 121–122, 127, 214, 223
fossils, 2, 4, 18–19, 21, 29–35, 39, 104, 128, 217, 226

of early hominins, 39
trace, 226
free will, 65, 95–96, 105, 111, 165–171, 174n10, 216, 217, 219

Galapagos Islands, 24
Garden of Eden. *see* Eden
Gemarah, 15n5, 58
genes, 3, 23, 36–38, 107, 129, 217, 218, 221
Genesis, 1–2, 5–7, 9–14, 19, 24–25, 27n8–n9, 30, 32, 53–68, 73, 79,
    82n8, 83n12, 85–86, 89, 91, 93–97, 104–105, 116, 121, 134, 136–
    149, 152n45, 154–156, 169, 177–194, 199, 215, 216, 220, 224, 225.
    see also specific days
    as information source, 54–57
    interpreting, 53–68
    King James Version, 5, 177–194
    Ramban on, 64–65
Genesis Flood, 14, 22, 60, 107, 118, 131, 141, 143, 147–148, 205–
    206, 208–209, 217, 222
The Genesis Flood, 22
Genesis Rabbah, 59–60
genetics, 13, 19–20, 29, 36–38, 132, 217
genome(s), 29, 36–38, 217, 218
genus, 9, 39, 218
geology, 17–18, 27n8, 210n4, 222
Gichon river, 86
God, 1, 3–13, 18, 22–23, 25–27, 55, 57, 64–65, 68, 71–73, 77–78, 79,
    82n11(2), 83n12, 85–86, 89–91, 93, 95–96, 104–106, 111–120,
    125n14, 129, 132–133, 137, 139, 143, 145, 153–155, 165, 169–170,
    177–194, 197, 202
    anger of, 116–117
    as architect of human life, 4–5
    as conscious observer, 11, 12, 77, 83, 105
    creation of human life by, 1, 5–6, 54
    creation of universe and life by, 1–2, 215, 226
    creative process, 114–118, 219
    essential name of, 112–114, 132–133, 178n2
    moment(s), 115–118, 120, 125n14, 213
    names of, 113–115, 132, 222
    Word of God, 5, 8, 22, 91
Goodall, Jane, 91–92, 105, 219
Gospel, 7

Gould, Stephen Jay, 23, 47n4, 47n5(ii)
grammar, 45–46, 159
Great Shabbat, 82n8
Great Synagogue, 57
Greeks, ancient, 17, 107
ground water discharge, 147–148, 208–209

Ham, 154–156, 160–162, 184, 186, 190–192, 217
Hamito–Semitic languages, 160
Havayah, 113
Hebrew, 17, 54–55, 58, 65, 93, 97, 108, 113, 115, 133, 135, 145–146,
    153, 156, 195
Hillel, 61
history
    earth, 98n14
    Homo sapiens, 29
    human, 8, 12–14, 35, 37, 43, 54, 60, 131–132, 148–149, 154,
        162, 171–173
    of language, 159–162
Holocene Impact Working Group, 207
Holy Bible. *see* Bible; scriptures; specific books
hominid(s), 1, 9, 37, 39–40, 217–218
hominin(s), 9, 21, 23, 34–35, 39, 43, 45–46, 103, 107, 127, 218
hominoid(s), 109, 217–218
Homo, 41, 43, 44,
    genus of, 9, 39, 218
Homo erectus, 40, 44–45, 50n29
Homo habilis, 43, 44–45, 50n29
Homo sapiens, 1, 4, 9, 12, 14, 29, 39–41, 44, 49n17, 73–74, 80, 90, 95,
    97, 103–109, 111–123, 127–129, 131, 140, 148, 153–154, 157, 159,
    162, 170–172, 213, 214, 218, 221
    appearance of, 12, 14, 29, 80, 111–123, 128
    Biblical vs. scientific account, 127–129
    definition of, 103, 127, 218
    mission of, 170–171
Hoshaiah, 59
human(s)
    anatomically modern, 9, 40, 44, 104, 109, 118, 120–121, 127–
        129, 131, 213
    appearance of, 6, 8, 10, 13, 39, 43, 65, 67, 73, 127
    behavioral modernity, 40–41, 119, 121–122, 129, 161, 214

behaviorally modern, 44, 104–105, 118, 120–121, 127–128, 131,
    153, 159, 162, 171–172, 214
creation of, 1, 5, 54, 58, 60, 91
differences between other primates and, 1,38, 90–91, 99n15
evolution of, 9–10, 13, 20–21, 25–26, 39
genome. *See* genome(s)
impact of Flood on, 14, 133, 148–149, 154
information from buried remains about, 29, 35, 37, 41,
intermediary between animals and, 21, 107–108, 219
language(s), 6, 12, 14, 41, 44–47, 50n28, 50n29, 103–104, 127–
    128, 132, 143, 149, 153–162, 220
lifetimes of, 91, 106–107, 122, 131
migrations of, 41–43
modern. *see* Homo sapiens
modern behaviors, 40–41, 104, 121, 123, 214, 221, 223
origins of, 2,–3, 8–11
population of, 1, 37, 127–128, 132, 172–173
scientific timeline for, 8–9
timeline, 38–47, 80–81
"human" (term), 39
Human Genome Project (HGP), 37–38, 218
humanity, 2–3, 8, 10–14, 17–, 22, 37, 54, 73–74, 91, 96, 103–109,
    129, 131, 139
Human Time, 12–14, 53, 56–57, 67–68, 72–73, 77–81, 82n11, 105,
    117–120, 199, 215, 216, 218
conversion from Creation Time to, 57, 67, 79, 82n11, 105
conversion from Divine Time to, 77, 81, 119
definition of, 218
end time, 78–79, 83
moment(s), 115–120, 213,
solar years, 68
start time, 78, 82n11
Human Timeline, 38–47, 80–81
Huxley, Thomas Henry, 21
hyoid bone, 45, 218

incarnate, 97, 103–104, 106, 118, 120–121, 123, 128, 153, 218
India, 86–87, 160, 208
Indo–European languages, 160, 162
information sources, 54–57
Injil, 7

intellectual soul, 95–97, 219
intelligent design, 24, 219
intermediary(ies), 21, 107–109, 219
Isaac ben Samuel of Acre, 12, 59, 67–69, 219
    Otzar HaChaim (Life's Treasure), 67–68, 199, 219, 223
    timeline of, 59, 67
Islam, 7, 25–26
Isotope(s), 31–32, 47n2, 219
Israel, 25–26, 58, 143, 146, 196–197, 202,

Japheth, 154–156, 160–162, 219
Jerusalem Talmud, 59
Jesus, 7
Jew(ish), 5, 7, 59, 65, 71, 82n2, 113, 195, 200, 215, 221, 225–226
Jochanan ben Zakkai, Rabban, 61
Joseph, 169–170, 174n10
Joshua, 57
Jubilee Year, 197–198, 219
Judaism, 2, 6–7, 61, 64, 220, 225

Kabbalah, 57, 65–67, 200, 213, 220, 226
Kah: name of God, 113
Kanzi (chimp), 45–46
Kaplan, Rabbi Aryeh, 12, 68, 198–199
Kel: name of God, 113
Kerem Shlomo on Etz Chaim, 200
knowledge: basis of, 3–8
kof, 108

Lamarck, Jean–Baptiste, 20
land subsidence, 87–88, 209
language(s), 1, 4–6, 12, 14, 41, 44–47, 50n28, 50n29, 54, 60, 63, 71–74, 91, 103–104, 123, 127–128, 132, 143, 145, 149, 153–162, 171, 210, 214, 220
    creation of, 91
    dispersion of, 156–157
    history of, 159–162
    human, 44–47
    Indo–European, 160
    proto–language, 156, 220
language families, 156,–157, 160–162, 220

Laplace, Pierre Simon, 18

Leviticus, 151n30, 196, 198, 200, 203n1–2, 203n4–5, 203n7

life, 1, 3–7, 17–18, 23–24, 26–27, 29–36, 66, 76, 79–81, 85–86, 90–94, 106–107, 115, 122, 135, 154, 201, 217, 220,
 creation of, 1, 5
 definition of, 220
 emergence of, 9, 34, 39,
 evidence preserved in fossil record, 13, 24, 29–31, 34–35, 37, 80, 214, 223
 sequence revealed in fossil record, 33–35
 timeline for appearance on earth, 34–35

light: behavior of, 166–168, 172, 226

Lithops, 107–108

lithosphere, 87, 207, 220, 223

long(er) life, 122–123, 131

Louisiana Balanced Treatment Act, 22, 220

Lubavitcher Rebbe (Menachem Mendel Schneerson), 122, 220

Lurianic Kabbalah, 67, 213

Luria, Rabbi Isaac (the Ari or Arizal), 59, 66–67, 96, 105, 107–108, 112, 198–200, 213

Maimonides, 71, 221

man. *see also* human(s)
 creation of, 5–6, 26, 55, 58, 64–65, 76, 81, 89, 90, 99n15, 112
 definition of, 74, 127
 in the image of God, 111–112, 219

mass extinction event. *see* extinction events

materialistic process, 20, 27n3, 222

Messianic age, 11, 221

meteorite(s), 206–209, 221

micro–evolution, 24

Midrash, 56, 58–59, 74, 79, 89–90, 93–94, 127, 140–141, 143, 221
 definition of, 58, 221
 description of the Flood, 140–143

Midrash Rabbah, 59–60, 79, 140, 221

Midrashim, 15n5, 57, 59–60, 86, 134, 137, 140

migration(s), 41–44, 149, 154, 161–162

Minoans, 209–210

Mishnah, 58, 61, 71, 108

modern human behavior, 40–41, 104, 121, 123, 214, 221, 223
 appearance and emergence of, 41, 120

definition of, 214
soul sparks of, 104–105
modernity, behavioral, 40–41, 119, 121–122, 129, 161, 214
moment(s), 115–118, 120, 125n14, 213
for Adam, 120
for God, 115–118, 120, 125n14, 213
moral struggle, 92–93
Moses, 5, 7, 15n4, 57, 59, 65, 116–117, 128, 202,
Five Books of, 5–7, 15n5, 59, 63–65, 96, 221, 225
timeline of, 59
Moses ben Nachman Girondi, Rabbi (Ramban). see Ramban
mountains, formation of, 87, 98n14
Muslims, x, 7, 15n4, 25
mystical tradition, 65–66, 133

Nahmanides (Ramban). see Ramban
names of God, 68, 113, 132, 222
National Human Genome Research Institute (NHGRI), 38
National Institutes of Health, 37–38
Native Americans, 210
natural selection, 1, 18, 20, 24, 219, 222
nature, 1, 4, 7, 17, 21, 24, 30, 55, 65, 66, 91, 132–133, 147, 166, 168,
Elokim and, 132–133, 147, 205–209, 216
mechanisms to produce the Flood, 149–148, 205–210
Neanderthals, 40, 44–46
nebular hypothesis, 18, 222
neo–Darwinian synthesis, 20, 22–23, 222
New Testament, 7
Noah, 60, 97, 104, 106, 116, 132–133, 135, 136–149, 153–157, 222
descendants of, 154–156
and the Flood, 133, 135–140, 145, 148–149
Noah's ark, 116, 133–139, 144, 148, 222

OEC. see old earth creationism
old earth creationism (OEC), 18, 25, 27n8, 222
Old Testament, 7
Omer, 195–196, 215, 222
On the Origin of Species (Darwin), 9, 18, 21–22
Oral Law, 7–8, 15n5, 53, 57–59, 65, 222, 225
interpretation of, 53, 57–62
key components of, 57–58

origins debate, 3, 17–26, 215, 222. *see also* creation–evolution
    controversy
Otzar HaChaim (Life's Treasure), 67–68, 199, 219, 223
Out of Africa or recent African origin hypothesis, 9–10, 40–43, 149,
    161, 223

paleontology, 17, 30, 223
Paul (Apostle), 7
Pentateuch (books of the Law), 5
physical cycles, 196–197,
Pirkê de Rabbi Eliezer (or "Chapters of Rabbi Eliezer"), 59–62, 137,
    223
Pishon river, 86
planning depth, 40
plants, 24, 30, 34–35, 81, 94, 107–108, 215, 217
plate tectonics, 87, 223
Pope Pius XII, 9–10
population, human, 1, 37, 127–128, 132, 172–173
Porta, Bonastrucça (Ramban). *see* Ramban
primate(s), 1–2, 9, 14, 35, 37, 39–40, 45, 91, 103, 105, 107–109, 127–
    128, 218, 221, 223
progressive creationists, 23, 223
Prophets, 5, 7, 15n5, 57
Protestants, American, 21–23
proto–language, 156, 220
Psalms, 6–7, 11, 15n5, 56, 77, 146

quantum mechanics, 11, 166, 224
Qur'an, 7

radioactive dating, 31–32, 224
radiometric dating. *see* radioactive dating
Ramban, 59, 62, 64–65, 67, 82n8, 111, 224
rank. *see* taxonomy
Rashi (Rabbi Shlomo Yitzhaki), 59, 62–64, 79, 111–112, 202, 224
religion, 1, 2–3, 6–9, 13, 23
    agreement with science, 8, 13
    basis of knowledge for, 3–8
    view of human origins, 9–11
Renaissance, 17–18

sabbatical cycles, 195–197, 199–200
Sabbatical Year, 196–198, 219, 225
Saudi Arabia, 25
Schneerson, Menachem Mendel. *see* Lubavitcher Rebbe
science, 2–3, 8, 10–13, 17, 20, 24–26, 29–47, 53–54, 65, 81, 119–120, 127–129, 161–162, 210n4, 224
    agreement with religion, 8
    basis of knowledge for, 3–8
    definition of, 224
    evidence for the Flood, 147–148
    record of history of language, 161–162
    time in, 11–13
    timeline for human origins, 8–9
    view of Homo sapiens, 127–129
scientific approach, 3–4, 173
scientific creationism, 22–23, 25, 224
scientific inquiry, 4, 17–21
scientific method, 1, 3–4, 8, 29–30, 225
scientific theory, 1, 9, 29, 54–55, 87, 127, 223
Scopes, John, 21
scripture(s), 2, 5, 7, 11, 15n4, 53–69, 113, 128, 171
semitic languages, 160
sequence of life, 33–35
7: cycles of, 195–198
70 nations, 153–154, 156, 158, 161–162, 225
Shaar HaGilgulim, 67, 105
Shabbat, 82n8
Shakai: name of God, 113
Shammai, 61
Shem, 154–156, 160–162, 225
Shimon bar Yochai, Rabbi, 65–66
Shmita (release), 196–198, 225
sin, 65, 73–74, 79–80, 85, 87, 89, 90, 92–97, 103–105, 109, 111, 118–120, 123, 129, 131, 153, 171
Sino–Tibetan languages, 161–162
Smith, William, 18
solar years. *see* Human Time
soul, 7–8, 10, 55, 65, 67, 74, 76, 81, 89–91, 93, 95–97, 103–107, 112, 115, 118–123, 128–129, 131–132, 148, 153, 170–173, 201, 204n18, 213, 219
    animalistic, 95–96, 213

intellectual, 95–96, 219
soul–elements of high rank ("upper light"), 96
soul roots, 96
soul spark(s), 97, 104, 106, 118, 120–121, 123, 128, 170–173
speciation, 109, 128, 225
speech and language, 44–47, 91. *see also* language(s)
spiritual cycles, 195–196
start time, 78, 82n11
storms, 133, 205
Sudan, 25
symbolic behavior, 40

Talmud, 7–8, 15n5, 16n13, 56–61, 63–64, 66, 73–74, 77, 79, 83n12,
    108, 195, 198, 202, 204n18, 225
    Babylonian, 15n5, 16n13, 58–59, 63, 83n12, 204n18
    employment rules for workers, 83n12
    Jerusalem, 59
Tawrat, 7
taxonomy, 225
Tennessee, 21
Tetragrammaton, 113
The Descent of Man (Darwin), 21
theistic evolution, 23–24, 27n8, 225
theory of evolution, 9, 18–19, 21–22, 24–25, 109
tikkun (rectification), 97, 106, 225
time, 10–14. *see also* Creation Time; Divine Time; Human Time
time conversion formula, 77
timelines, 1–3, 8, 10, 12–14, 24, 29, 34, 38–39, 43, 53–54, 56, 58–59,
    67, 73–74, 79–81, 89, 94, 97, 105, 109, 111, 118–120, 127, 195,
    198–200, 202, 215
    for appearance of animals, 33
    for appearance of clothing, 122
    for appearance of Homo sapiens, 12, 14, 29, 80, 111–123
    for appearance of humankind, humans and early actions, 6, 8–9,
        10, 14, 39, 43, 54, 65, 67, 73, 79,
    for appearance of life on earth, 29, 34, 80
    for appearance of plants, 108
    Bible–derived, 11–13
    of Biblical sources and persons, 59
    conversion of times, 71–81
    for creation, 73–76

for Day 6, 81, 202
differences among time measurements, 72
Divine, 200–200, 202
Human, 38–47, 80–81
scientific timeline for human origins, 8–9
sequence of life revealed in fossil record, 33–35
for the sin, 118–123
Titanic, 131, 139
Torah, 7–8, 11–13, 15n5, 53–54, 59, 63–64, 66, 71–72, 91–92, 109–
110, 112, 117–118, 127, 138, 157, 165, 169, 195–198, 202, 226
definition of, 225
on free will and divine providence, 169–170
interpreting, 53–54
Moses' receiving of, 117
timeline of, 59
trace fossils, 31, 226
Tree of Knowledge of Good and Evil, 106, 165
tsunami, 133, 147–148, 205–208, 210, 226
Turkey, 25, 137–138, 161
two–slit light wave interference, 166–168
Tzevakot:name of God, 113

United States, 23, 25, 214
universe: creation of, 1, 5, 7, 11
upper light (soul–elements of high rank), 96
U.S. Department of Energy, 37–38
U.S. Supreme Court, 22–23

Venus, 71
Vital, Rabbi Hayyim ben Joseph, 67–68
Vital, Shmuel, 67
volcanic eruptions, 87, 205–206, 226

Wallace, Alfred, 18, 226
wave–particle duality, 166–167, 226
Western Europe, 25
will, free. *see* free will
Word of God, 5, 8, 22, 91. *see also* God
workers: employment rules for, 83n12. *see also* Talmud
Written Law, 7–8, 53, 57, 63, 222, 224, 225

YHWH, 113, 133
Yitzhaki, Rabbi Shlomo. *see* Rashi
young earth creationism, 25, 27n8, 27n9, 226

Zabur, 7
Zohar, 7, 59, 65–67, 82n8, 222, 226

Made in the USA
Las Vegas, NV
22 February 2021